– ESSEX –
HEADLINES

Other Essex titles from Countryside Books include

GHOSTS OF ESSEX
Betty Puttick

THE LANDSCAPES OF ESSEX
Robert Hallmann

ESSEX TALES OF MYSTERY AND MURDER
W H Johnson

ESSEX OFF THE BEATEN TRACK
Stan Jarvis & Robert Hallmann

THE ESSEX VILLAGE BOOK
Federation of Essex Women's Institutes

ESSEX AIRFIELDS IN THE SECOND WORLD WAR
Graham Smith

-ESSEX-
HEADLINES

Stan Jarvis

COUNTRYSIDE BOOKS
NEWBURY BERKSHIRE

The front cover picture showing the Witham railway crash
is from a commercial postcard, courtesy of the
Nigel Bowdidge Collection

Typeset by Textype, Cambridge
Produced by MRM Associates Ltd., Reading
Printed by J. W. Arrowsmith Ltd., Bristol

Contents

Introduction

Through 30 years of researching, reading and writing about the fair county of Essex, and in the process of writing a history of the *Essex Chronicle* in 1989, I have come across many fascinating stories which had to be set on one side because they were not germane to the immediate and particular subject of my study.

Then Suzanne and Nicholas Battle gave me the opportunity to put some of those stories together under the title *Essex Headlines*. In the earlier days of the *Essex Chronicle*, which is proud of a record of continuous publication from 1764, there were headings, certainly, but all the stories included in this book would certainly have merited the more eyecatching' headlines of today.

For example, behaviour by sportsmen on the playing field certainly does not lead to murder today, as it did in 1776 in Tilbury, even though crowd behaviour is not always what it might be. Public safety standards are much more strictly enforced — you cannot fly your own home-made plane without the most rigorous examination of man and machine. The public attitude to the death penalty, as shown by its parliamentary representatives, has changed to tolerance and attempts at sympathetic understanding.

But these stories were not written to improve the mind. I recount them to show what pleasure can be had from delving into a great store of newspaper reports, court records, and the folklore for which the people of old Essex were celebrated. I do hope sincerely that people will have as much enjoyment in reading this book as I have had in its researching and writing.

So many people have given me help in the detailed investigation required to make this book as accurate as possible that it is not possible to mention them all by name. I trust that they will accept my thanks as expressed verbally, but there are those whose help has been crucial to the completion of this work, to whom I would like to put my gratitude in print.

The ever helpful staff and the unequalled resources of the *Essex Chronicle*. The staff of the Chelmsford Library and the Essex Record Office including my friends Anne Charles and Janet Gyford. My old friend in photography Ron Patient. My new friends Lisa Sibley and David Bartram, both of Essex County Council. Miss P.E.G. Wood and Mr Trevor Disley of Dolphyn Gallery, Coggeshall, who helped me with otherwise unobtainable photographs. Mr G.R. Bragg made a very helpful contribution from his St John Ambulance book of 1905.

Special thanks are given to two publishers who have allowed me to quote from their books: G.T. Foulis & Co. for *Henri Mignet and His Flying Fleas* by Ken Ellis and Geoff Jones under the imprint of the Haynes Publishing Group; and Macmillan Inc for *The Dangerous Skies* by A.E. Clouston.

Stan Jarvis

Earthquake!

★

Soon after nine o'clock on Tuesday morning, 22nd April 1884, there occurred the worst earthquake in England for 400 years. In 1480 Norfolk had borne the brunt of the upheaval. In 1884, when the whole of East Anglia was shaken, Essex was at the centre of the shock.

This great earthquake of 1884 was centred right on Abberton, just south of Colchester and its shocks were felt in a circle with a radius of some 180 miles — north-west at Altrincham, south-east at Ostead and south-west on the Isle of Wight. It has been claimed that this remains on record as the worst earthquake in British history with its effect felt over an area of 50,000 square miles.

They certainly felt it in Colchester. The station master, Mr W. Blatch, told how he was just going to start the 9.20 am up-express when '....there was a rumbling noise resembling distant thunder, and directly the platform seemed to give a gentle heave, like the motion of a wave. For an instant I thought I had a slight dizziness in the head, but then I was convinced that something unusual had happened, and that we were receiving either the shock of an explosion or an earthquake. The passengers in the train all rushed alarmed to the windows of the carriages, and a number of men at work on the new asylum, a large building close to the station, hastened down from the scaffold.'

In the town many a chimney stack swayed and crashed down. Clocks by the score were stopped, with pendulums swinging backwards and forwards instead of side to side. That great landmark, the huge brick water tower on four legs, called Jumbo by the locals, supporting a tank containing a million gallons of water, was seen to lean perceptibly, but though its arches developed cracks the structure stayed intact. Disaster was just a few degrees on the Richter scale away. Just out of town that much-visited tourist attraction Bourne Mill looked in a very sorry state after the shock passed. Its gable end had shifted a clear two inches.

Abberton, three and a half miles south of Colchester, was badly hit, situated as it was above the epicentre. Nearly every chimney was jolted down as rubble. Roofs were buckled and walls were cracked. The Lion inn's chimney stack toppled through the roof, and miraculously only one glass in the bar was shattered. The new rectory, which was then still in the course of construction, was damaged in every room. The churches of the three Layer villages — Breton, Marney and De-La-Haye — were damaged to a greater or lesser degree, but it was at Langenhoe that the worst damage to a church occurred, so bad in fact that it could not be used again and was never rebuilt. Langenhoe Hall had most of its roof shaken off. At Peldon the battlements of the church tower fell through the roof of the nave and its walls were cracked and shifted out of position. The church tower at Wivenhoe developed a crack half its height from the top. The shock caused the turrets to break away completely. The Chapel in West Street was also much damaged, inside and out. Quay House had all its chimneys collapse and its back wall bulged so alarmingly that it had to be rebuilt. The builder set the momentous date of 1884 in the new wall where it can still be seen today.

The duration of the tremor varied greatly from the centre to the fringes of the earthquake. At its centre around Langenhoe an observer quoted a period 'not less than 20 seconds'. In Colchester it was said to have lasted eight seconds and by the time it had spread to Chelmsford the shaking lasted for five seconds. The effect of this earthquake on the people of the time is best expressed in the language of the local paper of the day:

'The shock was felt at 20 minutes past nine o'clock in nearly every part of Essex, and various surmises were rife through-

Damaged houses at Wivenhoe, after the worst earthquake in England for 400 years.

out the morning as to the cause. In Colchester, indeed, very little doubt could exist as to the cause, for there the destruction of property was so great that nothing short of an earthquake or a tremendous explosion could have brought it about, and, upon it being ascertained that there had been no explosion, the terrified inhabitants of the town knew they had experienced a shock of earthquake. But in other places where the disturbance was less severely felt, individuals, until they found their experience confirmed by that of others, for the most part attributed their novel sensations to personal indisposition or to other circumstances of a general nature. Upon notes being compared, however, it was concluded that an earthquake or an explosion had occurred, and in the course of the morning we received several telegrams from several places inquiring as to the cause of the shock. Very naturally there was much excitement in all the places affected, and at Chelmsford the offices of this journal were besieged throughout the day by people reading the telegrams displayed in the windows. At Colchester the excitement was from the first of the most intense description. People ran out of their houses into the street, some of them partially clothed, and there was great consternation until it was seen that the danger was past.'

A survey of the damage in Colchester included the spire of the Lion Walk Congregational chapel which became just a pile of rubble down in the graveyard. The rumbling noise which accompanied the subterranean movement was described by people well away from the noises of the town as like the distant booming of a great gun. At Maldon the shock was not so severely felt, but the strange thing was that the greatest effect of the shock waves was felt in the strongest building in town — the old Moot Hall. In that part of it occupied by the police station, Head Constable Wombwell and PC Parrott were working quietly away when they were alarmed by a great crash at the back of the building and an 'apparent upheaving of the whole pile.' They were in no doubt that the place was about to collapse on top of them, so they ran out into the High Street, only to find scores of folks from shops and houses doing exactly the same.

They found afterwards that the great crash they had heard was the violent collision of the two great weights of the town clock, which, despite this, kept on ticking for another half an hour before giving up the ghost. Half the house-bells in the town were set a-jangling and plates and pots went flying in kitchens where, as the reporter humorously put it, 'good things were done for the earthenware dealers!' The only casualty in all the town was a baby whose high chair was toppled over by the vibrations, but he was not hurt a bit, bless his little heart!

In Chelmsford the effect of the earthquake was recorded by one inhabitant as follows: 'Houses of the largest, as well as those of the most limited dimensions were shaken bodily, people were almost transferred from their seats to the ground, cups and saucers rattled, and in some cases were overthrown,

Repairing the earthquake damage at Wivenhoe. A fund was raised for the relief of the many poor people who found themselves unable to pay for the substantial repairs required.

door bells rang, doors were rattled, and in various other ways people were disturbed by the violence of the convulsion. Throughout the day the one engrossing topic of conversation in the town was the commotion it had produced and its probable cause.' Though some people had felt a strange giddiness from this 'momentary oscillation', they did not associate that condition with the unusual ringing of the bells when no-one was there. They had not been involved in an earthquake before, so that bell-ringing took on the quality of a wierd psychic manifestation — until at last the true explanation, by the end of the day, had been circulated.

One classic reaction to the event has been preserved for us. Mr Gaywood the butcher was chatting to a friend outside his shop when he suddenly broke off with, 'Hullo! There's my meat dancing about. Whatever's amiss with-it?' All the car-cases and joints in those days were hung on hooks in the unglazed shop 'window' and the tremor had set them all swinging. The newspaper could report a truly eye-witness account of what effect the earthquake had on the offices of the *Essex Chronicle*: 'At the office of this paper much consternation was caused among the employees. One of them was so startled that he rushed out of a lower room to see if anything had occurred to the boiler, while those employed in the upper rooms were alarmed by the extraordinary vision of the building swaying quite perceptibly.... In another of the rooms the shock was felt in a series of three or more waves, the wall was distinctly heard to crack, the floor was visibly depressed, and the outside wall and a table looked as if they were about to be precipitated into Mr W. Dennis's yard [adjoining]'.

At a distance from the centre, places like Chigwell Row, Clacton and Horndon-on-the-Hill reported a slight shock. A very good description of the sensation felt by thousands of people was penned by Mr G.F. Beaumont of Coggeshall: 'I was sitting in my dining room with my wife and two other ladies, on the morning of 22nd April 1884, when we all suddenly experienced an oscillation similar to that which would result from the passing of an express train through a railway-station.... the glass back of my sideboard which faces east oscillated, and was the object which most attracted our attention... From enquiries I have made of the leading inhabitants of this town I find that in most of the houses the bells rang more or less, but in some instances violently. In many cases also clocks stopped.... I have not heard of any well in this neighbourhood in which the water has been affected.'

Chimneys, lofty structures most at risk in an earthquake, were toppled miles away from the epicentre. At Dedham, on the county border, the Hall, the Marlborough Hotel and the Gun inn lost their stacks. Pendulum clocks stopped at 9.18 precisely. At Frating, some two and a half miles north-east of Wivenhoe a house called Frating Abbey, only some 40 years old, had all its chimneys so shaken that they had to be supported straight away. At Great Bentley the old windmill was severely shaken, making the miller rush out in a panic. The damage was so great that it could not be used again. It was taken down altogether in 1891.

Colonel Arthur S. Lowe of Gosfield Hall wrote his account of what happened in that parish: 'The vibratory motion lasted about ten seconds, during which the absence of wind was remarkable, and all phenomena carefully noted at once proclaimed it an earthquake shock. Our old hall shook on the S. and E. sides with undulatory motion, many of the floors and walls apparently upheaving and subsiding with manifest agitation, the pictures in the different rooms bulging forward and shaking in their frames: the lake was tremulous with an upheaving oscillation; clocks stopped (facing the E.) and glass clattered everywhere.... No structural damage was done at Gosfield, and no individual out of doors seemed to feel like those within.'

Many a person, like Mr Cockey of Rettendon, was amazed to see the pictures swinging on the wall. Without radio or television the mystery was not solved until they opened their newspaper on the following morning. At Southminster villagers were surprised to hear two of the church bells clang out just once — the vicar was more aggrieved than surprised for three of the vicarage chimneys were so cracked that they had to be rebuilt. The vicar of Stebbing neatly summed up the sensations of thousands of people well away from the epicentre: '....There was time for expressions of surprise and remarks that it must be either an earthquake or dynamite. The floor of the room was felt to rise and sink as the deck of a ship which meets a wave. There was a rumbling sound. Everything in the room moved; the curtains waved to and fro. A lady sitting in a chair was moved up and down, one leg of the chair rapping the floor as long as the shock lasted.... The pictures swayed on the wall.... The whole house, which is crazily built, shook and rattled. The shock was not felt at all by the gardener, who was in the coach-house at the time.... I find that, generally speaking, people out of doors did not feel it. No damage was done in this place.'

A sense of anti-climax is engendered by the report that a parrot in Kelvedon and a cockatoo in Maldon were both affected by the earthquake — they fell off their perches!

Within a week a public subscription had been put in hand and the Lord Mayor of London had been asked to open a fund for the relief of the many poor people who, though owning their own cottages, did not have the wherewithal to pay for the substantial repairs required.

Another view of the reason for the earthquake was put forward by the preacher at a Congregational church in the county town on the following Sunday. He postulated that the effects experienced proved this was an earthquake and some people said it was certain evidence that the world would shortly be coming to an end for there was the text that said 'There shall be earthquakes in divers places' at the second coming of Our Lord. The preacher, himself, thought seriously that this earthquake was the herald of the certain ultimate destruction of the world. 'The fires are already kindled underneath our feet. They are just waiting for the touch of the finger of God, and the work will be done.... Those volcanic eruptions are evidence of these fires which will at last burst forth and consume the globe.' These were hardly words of comfort and hope to a congregation which had just suffered a very nasty shock! In contrast we can read of thanksgiving services being held at the various places of worship in Coggeshall '....for preservation from the recent earthquake'. It is true that not one life was lost.

The Biggest Street Party In The World

The biggest and the earliest street party held in Essex must surely be that which took place in Chelmsford on 19th July 1821. It was not just any old street, it was the main street in Chelmsford, the High Street — and it was completely closed to traffic all day. It had to be a very important celebration to justify such an extreme step — it was the day of the coronation of King George IV.

It is a little surprising that the people of Chelmsford should get so excited about the event for King George, as Prince Regent from 1812, had been King in all but name for the past 18 years and he had not been all that popular. On his 50th birthday in 1821 Leigh Hunt, the poet and essayist, described him as, 'A libertine over head and ears in debt and disgrace, a despiser of domestic ties, the companion of demi-reps [people with a bad reputation], a man who has just closed half a century without a single claim on the gratitude of his country or the respect of posterity.' Hunt was fined and imprisoned for the libel, but this was not the only mud thrown at the King and some of it stuck — quite fairly.

Obviously this opprobrium was not shared by the loyal and loving inhabitants of Chelmsford. They definitely wanted to show their pleasure, issuing a special statement beginning: 'It having been determined, by the Committee appointed to manage the celebration of the Coronation of King GEORGE the FOURTH, at Chelmsford, on the 19th July, 1821, that the several acts of Benevolence to the Poor, the List of Contributors, as well as the general Festivities, amongst the inhabitants, and their highly respectable neighbours, should be made a matter of record....'

This 'Record', in flowery language too rich for modern tastes, opens with a panegyric on the old King, George III and his Queen. It continues, 'Upon the demise of such a monarch, the people could not fail to cast their eyes on the object who was to succeed him. Already had George the Fourth given ample proof, while Regent, of his power and capacity to rule over a free people.' It concludes with a paragraph reciting the town's personal reasons for celebration. 'That the spirit of loyalty, animating so large a portion of the great and good of this nation, should have reached the ancient town of Chelmsford, is not to be looked upon as an extraordinary event; but in the expression and exercise of it, there appears something worth recording. This town has long been, and it is much to be hoped will ever continue its predominant attachment to the Constitution. It shared from this cause, in the year 1552, the munificence of a good and charitable Monarch (King Edward the Sixth) who established and endowed a valuable Free Grammar School within it, while probably the same motives introduced the returning Members to the Great Council at Westminster. We have also a pledge in our present Sovereign, of his wishes to promote our amusement, as well as our happiness, by his generous revival of the Hundred Guineas given annually at the Chelmsford Races, by his late Royal Mother Queen Charlotte; whereby much pleasure is afforded to all classes in the county, and no inconsiderable benefit to the town.... the present inhabitants'.... only ambition being, that, as an ancient and free town, their sentiments of genuine loyalty, plainly and unequivocally expressed, should be handed down to posterity, and that their children's children should shout, with heart-felt zeal, LONG LIVE OLD ENGLAND'S KING!'

So the arrangements for the street party went ahead. The first thing to do of course, was to form a committee. An anonymous local worthy sent a circular to the fathers of the town, calling them to a meeting, '....to consider and propose

Chelmsford High Street on 19th July 1821, the day of the coronation of King George IV. A bullock was roasted at the end of the street and around 1,500 people sat down to roast beef and plum pudding, washed down with 216 gallons of ale.

such measures as might be most conducive to promote the hilarity of the scene, and display, with that promptness and alacrity (which this town has ever been justly celebrated for), those decided marks of attachment towards their Sovereign, that on all occasions distinguishes the TRUE-BORN ENGLISHMAN!' It took place on 29th June at the Shire Hall and the most exhaustive rules and regulations were drawn up, appointing a management committee of 13 people.

The main points of the projected programme for the great day were: the roasting of a whole bullock at one end of the High Street; to have as many poor people as possible sitting down to a dinner at tables placed all down the middle of that same street; to have a public dinner 'for the gentlemen of the town and their friends' — admission by ticket only; a grand firework display; and then a general promenade around the town to enjoy the 'general illumination', which will be explained later. The Committee met frequently, with a great sense of urgency. They resolved that the poor people of Chelmsford would be informed of their bonanza by the Town Crier and printed handbills to tell them that if they handed in their names at the workhouse they would be given a ticket entitling them to a free Coronation dinner. No child under the age of seven would be allowed to attend, but 'such of the POOR as may prefer to be at HOME with their families, instead of dining on the 19th, ...will be allowed the same proportion of meat and beer as those who attend in public ....'

Mr Wenden, the butcher, was to find a good bullock at a sum not exceeding £15. Mr James Butler was to advise 'on the cookery of the said bullock'. Mr Coates, the timber merchant, offered to lend enough 'deals' to provide tables for at least 1,500 people to sit at. All the Chelmsford butchers were to share in the provision of meat for the dinner, in the same proportions as the subscriptions they had made to the fund! It was to be washed down with 216 gallons of ale from Chelmsford brewers under the same arrangement as the butchers. The bakers too were to benefit, for everybody at the dinner was to be provided with a three-halfpenny loaf of their very own.

With three days to go before the big event Sir John Tyrell, *the* local big-wig, declared he would make himself available on the day 'to meet the inhabitants of the town, and their friends' at dinner at four o'clock in the County Room of the Shire Hall. Tickets were 15 shillings each — the price of a *very* good dinner in those days. A special advertisement was placed in the Chelmsford newspaper to let everybody know just what to expect in the way of entertainment. At midnight the great day was to be ushered in by the firing of four cannon and the ringing of the Church bells for exactly an hour. At the moment they stopped the bullock would be put to the fire. As soon as it was light the tables were to be set up from the Shire Hall down to the Black Boy, just a step from the Stone Bridge. The Poor People had to take their own knives, forks, plates or trenchers and mugs. They were to be shepherded by members of the Committee, each of whom had undertaken

20

A contemporary print showing Chelmsford from Springfield Hill.

to find nine friends to help them. They also had to provide a tablecloth 84 ft long and the necessary serving dishes. As you can guess the innkeepers were over-run with requests for the loan of their cloths and utensils. Each group of Poor People, 100 strong, was told to assemble in a different part of the town, in inn yards, at the charity school, the workhouse, and so on. From there, at a given signal, the roar of a cannon at noon, they were to be led, like little armies, to take their places at the tables in the High Street, to 'begin at one o'clock upon the old English fare of roast beef and plum pudding.' Some 644 hot, boiled plum puddings, each weighing five lbs, had been ordered from Mr Wiffen.

When that dinner had been tucked away and the band had played *'God Save the King'*, a blast from a bugle brought the gorged and grateful poor folk to their feet to give three hearty cheers. Whether this was for the Committee, the contributors or for King George himself is not quite clear. And after that, if anybody was still hungry there was the roast bullock, cooked

21

to perfection over the smoking embers, doled out freely to the citizens who crowded round between three and four o'clock. Meanwhile the Committee members and their helpers were frantically working to clear away every table in the street, and every last utensil and tablecloth. They were anxious that they should not be late for the other dinner provided for the 'Gentlemen' and what a grand affair that was.

'Tables surrounded by upwards of 100 leading gentlemen of the neighbourhood, and the principal inhabitants of the town ....The viands and wine were truly excellent ....The band attended in the orchestra, and during the repast, enlivened the company with several popular airs ....the Chairman rose, and, in an impressive address, introduced the health of his gracious Majesty, King George the 4th, with four times four, which was received with long and loud acclamations.... the convivial spirit of the afternoon was kept up and enlivened by several admirable and constitutional songs, sung by gentlemen amateurs.' So went the reports — can't you just imagine it?

After that, at nine o'clock, came the fireworks, so remarkable that they brought forth this report: '....nothing of this kind, in our memory, had been offered to their view of such a splendid character.... — the flights of rockets — the brilliant effect of the Bengal and Chinese lights — the tasty evolutions of the various wheels — the tremendous explosion of the Jerbs and Mines.... was a superb treat....' When the fireworks were finished the darkness seemed even blacker for a few minutes until, at another signal, candles and oil lamps were lit in the windows of most of the shops and houses in the town — coloured lights and transparencies lit from behind made brilliant technicolour displays with patriotic mottoes clearly reflected. They were called 'illuminations' and the townsfolk promenaded round, enjoying this unusual sight, and the fact that beer had been distributed to points along the way.

The ashes of the roast bullock were stirred into another grand bonfire around which the people gathered to talk over the day's happenings and to marvel at the ingenuity of all the arrangements. Long after midnight there were still folk parading the town, singing, most enthusiastically, the national anthem. Yet there was absolutely no trouble — '....though so many thousands of persons were brought from their homes and occupations, and placed amidst scenes of merriment and glee, not the slightest tumult, insult, or party feeling was distinguished ....' in the less colourful, more limited language of our day, the newspaper might have summed it up, 'A good time was had by all'.

The Wonder Of The Age

This story of the Chelmer and Blackwater canal begins on 2nd June 1797, when the *Chelmsford Chronicle* reported, 'The navigation from Collier's Reach, to this town, being completed, all the barges now ready with coals etc, will, on Saturday morning, arrive at the last lock, in Springfield Mead, and at ten o'clock proceed in a grand procession, with colours flying, etc, into the Basin, near Springfield Bridge, the ground around, which is now divided and let to different persons for wharfs, will in a few days after the opening, be plentifully stored with coals, lime, chalk, cinders, etc, etc.' What a history of argument, effort, setbacks and disappointment, technical expertise and ultimate success lies behind this brief report.

The canal ran inland from Heybridge on the Blackwater to the county town of Chelmsford and its terminus in the neighbouring parish of Springfield. Heybridge had been chosen for the connection with the coastal trade because Maldon businessmen were afraid that if ships off-loaded into barges at their port the bulk trade would be straightway transferred to Chelmsford, much to their disadvantage. Yet there had been a time a hundred years earlier when Maldon men were much in favour of a canal.

In 1681 Andrew Yarranton, writing the second part of his *England's Improvement by Sea and Land to Outdo the Dutch Without Fighting*, pointed out that the local supplies of timber for Maldon's shipbuilding industry had been so depleted that a canal from Chelmsford to Maldon would be a most economical way of tapping the forests further to the west, like Waltham and Hatfield. He surveyed the course of a projected canal and reckoned it could all be done, including compensation to the

The first lock on the canal at Heybridge Basin.

water millers, for £8,000. There were not enough far-sighted investors to put up the money.

A more realistic scheme was propounded in 1732 when surveyor Hoare stated that the river Chelmer itself could be made navigable for just over £9,000, though a 'new cut', a canal, at nearly £13,000 was recommended. The interest this time came not from Maldon to ship in timber, but from Chelmsford to get all kinds of basic bulk supplies quickly and easily inland from colliers and coastal merchantmen. Maldon was much against it: it was dropped. Another very determined effort was made in 1762, largely by county gentlemen and Chelmsford businessmen. Thomas Yeoman was asked to draw up a report with a plan of the canal's course. There was a great division of opinion. Sir Henry Mildmay, lord of the manor of Chelmsford and owner of much of the land through which the Chelmer runs, was all for it, but another great land and mill owner, who later became MP for Maldon, was against it, fearing the loss of tolls which the port of Maldon was then able to charge on goods landed there.

The emergence of Chelmsford as the county town from the earliest days meant that by the middle of the 18th century it was a great centre of trade and industry; proponents of the canal scheme felt that Chelmsford should have its connection with the sea and shipping despite Maldon's opposition. Those Maldon merchants would see their town bypassed and their trade diminished as the canal took barge-loads of goods from coastal shipping in the basin below Maldon, including vast quantities of coal, chalk, lime and gravel needed by the towns and villages in the hinterland of Chelmsford. A separate source of opposition was the millers using the flow of the Chelmer to earn their bread and butter. By this scheme six mills or more would be put out of commission.

After the survey in 1762 the Chelmsford backers had Yeoman produce another plan in 1765, modified to gain greater support. The plan did not get approval, but the movement grew stronger through the years until the final, successful Chelmer and Blackwater navigation scheme was introduced in 1793. The time was ripe; canal-building was at its peak. In three years from 1791, 81 canal schemes were approved by Acts of Parliament. There was enough enthusiasm over this new wonder of the age to carry through many a scheme less well thought out than this one.

Around 1790, 6,250 tons of coal shipped from Newcastle were being sold throughout the Chelmsford district, and shortages were being experienced even then simply because the horse transport overland from Maldon and the condition of the roads did not allow any greater flow. The town's own population had more than doubled in 60 years, so demand was definitely outstripping supply. The preamble to the Bill put before Parliament for its approval said, '....as fuel can only be procured at a heavy expense from Maldon, Battlesbridge or [with London port duty added] from the Stortford Canal, and that manure [the marl or chalky clay obtained from

Purfleet or over in Kent] is at too high a price to be obtained in sufficient quantities, little doubt can arise, but that the operations of the canal will be such as to secure some tolerable profit to the Speculators....'

Maldon, on the other hand, was losing its significance as a port. One of several reasons was the silting up of the Blackwater estuary. It was only at spring tides that vessels over 50 tons burthen could be got up to the Fullbridge and the quays there. So it was in August 1792, that the promoters of the canal were able to announce their intention to introduce a Bill into Parliament '.... for making navigable the Rivers Chelmer and Can from the Port and Town of Maldon.... to the Town of Chelmsford.' The plan put forward showed a new channel to be made from Colliers Reach on the Blackwater estuary back up to Heybridge, then the river Blackwater was to be used to a point opposite Beeleigh Mill where another excavation would form a link with the Chelmer. The Can did not actually appear in the final plan. The famous John Rennie, who would act as supervising engineer, thought it could all be done for £30,000, including the building of four bridges.

The Maldon faction continued its opposition, but to no avail. The Bill received the Royal Assent on 17th June 1793. Chelmsford folk were almost over-enthusiastic on hearing the news. They set the church bells pealing, bonfires were lit in the streets and barrels of beer were brought out to dispense celebratory toasts to the proposers and to the success of the canal.

The Act allowed for the appointment of a hundred or so Commissioners to be referees in cases of dispute in the course of excavations for the canal and the introduction of locks and weirs. But John Rennie was far too busy a national figure to be always on the scene; he appointed Richard Coates as resident engineer, and it was he who gave the newly established company reports of progress at their regular meetings in the Black Boy, Chelmsford. He was a good man to have, for he was an experienced canal-builder. When he had seen through the completion of the Chelmer and Blackwater Navigation he

Some of the original brick canal bridges still remain, such as this one at Beeleigh, built in 1795.

and his brother George showed their confidence in its future by buying a site on the wharf at Springfield and importing coal, lime, chalk, timber and grindstones for selling on throughout the district. The business thrived.

More bridges than expected had to be built as the canal cut through fields and across existing roads. Some of those simple but elegant brick bridges are still in use. Work was started in the autumn of 1793, but there were unexpected difficulties of great variety to be overcome. Take one example. Mr Westcombe, owner of Langford Mill and land all round it, had already made a short length of canal from the mill on the Blackwater down to the Chelmer, which was called the Langford Cut by the locals. By July 1793, it needed only the lock to let it down to the level of the Chelmer. The new canal required the deepening of his canal by two ft to coincide with the level at which the company was operating. Westcombe fought his corner through the courts and got the compensation he was seeking. The company also had to fight off plans by Maldon businessmen to alter the final course of the canal so that ships would dock at *their* quays rather than at Heybridge Basin, but they lost, and at Heybridge and Springfield the wharves and landing and loading facilities were soon under erection including 'cranes and other engines'.

Lock-keepers' cottages were built near locks by the mills so that the flow of water could be fairly regulated for miller and bargee alike. The last of these cottages still existing can be seen at Hoe Mill. The excavation of the canal had crept from Heybridge to Boreham by April 1796. To take advantage of its potential as soon as possible a coalyard was set up at Boreham and, on 23rd April, barges at Heybridge were loaded with coal out of the brig *Fortune's Increase*, down from Sunderland, and towed up the new canal by horses to that coalyard. From there the coal was taken in horse-drawn wagons, all bedecked in ribbons to Chelmsford. The whole process from the arrival of the brig to the dumping of the coal on the wharf at Springfield took six days. At the same time the busy Hoe Mill had sent 150 sacks of flour down the canal to Heybridge for shipment on to London. By 5th September the canal had been dug out and the Chelmer suitably prepared to within three quarters of a mile of Chelmsford. There was much excavation to be undertaken over some months to establish the wider waters for the dock and the wharves at Springfield. It all went as smoothly as these big undertakings do and so at last we come to the report with which our story was begun, when, on 2nd June 1797, the full length of the Chelmer and Blackwater Navigation was complete and clear for traffic and trade.

But the company's trouble did not end there. Very heavy rain at the beginning of December 1797 completely swamped stretches of the canal and caused considerable silting up so that barge traffic was suspended while urgent repairs were effected. Chelmsford's new-found reserves of coal on the

Springfield wharf quickly vanished. It certainly brought home to the company and the town alike how important the Chelmer and Blackwater Navigation now was in everyone's daily life. Businesses blossomed on its banks because raw material and finished goods could be imported and sent away in bulk which made road transport look ineffectual.

For 45 years the company flourished through its golden period. In the last year of that period, 1842, no less than 60,000 tons of cargo was taken up and down the canal in barges. Then the railways came and the canal was made largely redundant, though timber was still being imported by barge right down to recent times. The rather bitter irony of the situation in that last great year of 1842 was that the company was doing well out of bringing up the river all kinds of heavy materials and gear for the extending of the railway from Brentwood through Chelmsford and on to Colchester.

The canal had a terrific effect on life throughout its length. The towpath gave such easy access to places along its banks that riders used it to the extent that the company often had to make repairs not just to the paths, but to the gates and fences which were broken down to gain access. Children found new bathing places, diving into the locks was no end of fun. Even adults did not heed the dangers of the new cuts. The local newspaper reported in January 1799:

'A private in the Surrey Regiment of Militia was drowned in our navigable canal so long ago as Saturday se'nnight, but the body was not found until the Saturday following. It appears that the deceased was skating and reading at the same time, when just below Mr Marriage's [mill], the continual stream coming from the mill into the navigable Cut, caused the ice to be so thin as not to bear the weight, but broke in with him. A person in the mill missed the deceased on a sudden, but supposing him to have quitted the ice, thought no more of it, until, enquiry being made, he gave such information as to lead to the discovery of the body. The deceased in his last moments seems to have made great efforts to save his life, the ice being much broken round the spot, but the place was again frozen over.' The poor soldier was buried with full military honours in Springfield churchyard on 14th January, 1799.

Now there is only one barge left on the canal, and that has been motorised and refitted to provide leisurely cruises down a waterway which has changed from a busy industrial artery to a peaceful, watery haven for wildlife. Let the leaflet advertising these cruises have the last word:

'The Canal Company's history is a fascinating one. From early commercial success in the late 18th and early 19th centuries, by providing a waterway for barges bringing coal, lime, timber and other goods towards Chelmsford from the coast, and taking flour from the various mills to the port at Heybridge, it met the challenge of the Railways stoically in the mid 19th century. Since then it has diversified by buying various riverside properties for investment, growing willows for the expanding cricket bat industry, and developing Heybridge Basin as a yachting centre. Now it is deeply involved in the leisure industry by providing boating and cruising facilities as a public amenity, and the cruiser *Victoria* is one of the means of introducing these beauties of hitherto unknown Essex to an appreciative public.'

Horror On Horror

A murder is a horrible event. When it causes further death and injury it becomes a sickening tragedy. Just such a tragedy happened here in Essex in 1856. The scene of the crime was the estate of Sir John Tyrell, based on Boreham House. This grand place was built in 1728 for Benjamin Hoare, incorporating materials taken from the demolition of part of the famous New Hall, about a mile away on the other side of the highway from London to Colchester. Sir John Tyrell was the last surviving male member of a family which had walked with kings from the days of the Conqueror. When he died in 1877 the title became extinct. He was very much alive, however, and serving as a Member of Parliament, in February 1856 when he was awakened at three o'clock in the morning to be told that one of his gamekeepers had been shot dead.

The story goes back to Saturday, 16th February, when the gamekeepers, plagued by poachers, had kept watch from a small house in Duke's Wood. They heard them, but as they crept out to ambush them the poachers sensed something was up and raced out of the wood to Russell's Green. There, where they were safely off the Tyrell property, they fired off their shotguns in sheer defiance of the keepers' efforts to catch them. They had not shot the birds they wanted, however, so the keepers knew they would come back. The watch was continued.

On Monday night, 18th February, at half past eleven, keepers Hales and Wisbey, and the latter's son, went creeping through the wood. The sound of shots an hour later confirmed their suspicions. They calculated just where the poachers were and had a whispered discussion on a plan of action. William Hales would circle round behind them and

32

An engraving showing Boreham House around 1830, home of Sir John Tyrell and scene of a murder in 1856.

make enough noise to drive them on into range of the Wisbeys who would stay where they were. Within two or three minutes they heard Hales call them loud and clear, 'Come on mates, here they are.' The Wisbeys rushed at once in the direction of that voice. They had hardly reached the denser wood from the glade where they had waited when they heard Hales cry, 'Oh, dear!' and a split-second afterwards came the flash and bang of a gun.

Unknown to them William Hales had received the full blast of shot, which killed him instantly. Two men came bursting through the dark wood, wild and desperate to make their escape. They almost ran straight into the Wisbeys but swerved at the last moment and split up. One ran back to the other side of the wood, and made his escape for the moment. The other man passed within a yard of young Wisbey, jinked away, and waded through a small pond; but Wisbey reacted so

33

quickly that he was right behind the poacher as he reached the edge of the pond. He made a flying tackle, grabbed the man, and Wisbey senior, crashing through the wood after them, came up at that moment to hit the poacher over the head with a stick, wrest his gun from him and throw it in the pond to render it useless.

The poacher gave in, and having been subdued, was taken to Duke's Lodge farmhouse nearby and there in the light of oil lamp and candles he was searched. They found in his pockets all the paraphernalia needed to produce home-made cartridges. There were small pieces of elder wood with the pith removed, stopped with a cork, to form cases which held a charge of gunpowder. In a dirty bag there was a quantity of lead shot. In another pocket was a quantity of home-made wadding. The man, who gave his name as James Thorogood, said he came from Fairstead. When they asked him if Hales was dead he replied, 'He fell like a dead man, certainly.' But he could not, or would not, at that time, say who fired that fatal shot.

The Wisbeys then took their prisoner back into the wood, to the spot where Hales had fallen. They found him there, dead alright, an appalling spectacle. The poor fellow could not have been more than three feet away from the gun when it was fired in his face. It was when he saw the muzzle thrust towards him from the black of the night that he must have exclaimed, 'Oh dear!' — the last words he spoke. He was sprawled on his back with his arms outstretched. His coat and shirt were still smouldering from the flame of the powder. They tried to brush off the ashes and to their horror the flames burst out again. Once they had dowsed them the corpse was carried out of the wood and into a cart which was driven to the dead man's cottage, where his wife and eight children were left to grieve.

By three o'clock in the morning Thorogood had been taken up to the Big House for an interview in the presence of Sir John Tyrell. Under hostile questioning he broke down and implicated his brothers William and Thomas, James Guiver and

Ebenezer Chalk as his partners in crime. This information brought swift action. A messenger was sent to police head-quarters at Springfield and Superintendents May and Raison were very soon at Boreham House, whilst Sergeant Simpson had a roving brief to look out for the suspects in Chelmsford. Superintendent May went on to Witham, picked up rein-forcements and went on to Fairstead. They found one of the Thorogood brothers in a field there, though it was not yet light, and took him in charge. They called on Chalk and found him in. They searched his house and found a wet jacket with pheasant's feathers stuck to it, powder and shot. In an outhouse, hidden away in two pieces they found the stock and barrel of a shotgun.

Superintendent Raison had been just as busy, going to Fuller Street and effecting the arrest of the third Thorogood and James Guiver, in whose house two loaded guns and a dead pheasant were found. All these men were young, Fairstead farm labourers. The Thorogoods, in contradiction of their name, already had a considerable prison record. Of Guiver an eye-witness said, 'Upon his apprehension and during his conveyance to gaol he treated the matter with considerable levity. He generally wears a cap, but when examined before the magistrate on Tuesday, he had almost a new hat on, hence it is inferred the cap picked up belongs to him.' Witnesses could confirm that on the previous evening all these men were seen in conversation at the beerhouse in Fuller Street and that they left it together.

The local paper sums up: 'For the promptitude and zeal displayed in the apprehension of these men the police deserve the greatest praise. They were informed of the affair about half-past three and by eleven or a little after the men were safely in their custody — another proof added to the many of the value of a well-organised system of police.'

That same Tuesday afternoon the suspects were taken before the Magistrate, Major Skinner, at the Shire Hall in Chelmsford. The word had spread like wildfire and the court was crowded. The evidence then put forward was Wisbey senior's

A print showing Chelmsford High Street in 1863, looking towards Shire Hall, where the four defendants were due to appear on Friday 22nd February.

testimony and James Thorogood's own admission. The prisoners were remanded to the county gaol to appear again on the following Friday at noon.

The next step was the Coroner's Inquest held at 7 pm at Duke's Farm, though the jury went to Mr Hales' cottage first to view the body. They saw most of his face covered in blood and blackened by the burning powder. The charge of the shot had been fired so close that its entry into the base of the neck made only a small hole, no bigger than a penny. Part of the man's neckcloth had been forced into it and the clothes across his chest had been completely burned away. Joseph Bragg Wisbey gave his evidence of the action on what he called '....a moonlight night but not very bright.' On such a night it was impossible to see any really distinctive features or colours. He did find a light-brown cap which tangled boughs had brushed off a man's head in his wild attempt to escape.

Joseph Wisbey, junior, a carpenter, said that Thorogood when he was caught said, 'Don't hurt me, I've hurt no-one:

I told my mates before we came out not to shoot anyone if likely to be taken; I fired only once.' He denied he had shot Hales, 'I have only shot my gun off once; my gun is not loaded.' Wisbey continued: 'I said no more to him then until we got to Duke's Lodge, when I asked the reason why his gun was not loaded. He said, "I had not had time to load it; I wanted to get away".' A juror asked Thorogood what he had fired at and was told it was a pheasant, which fell into the water — but no such pheasant had been found. At half-past ten that night the inquest was adjourned to the Cock inn at Boreham on the Saturday following. Then Mr C.O. Copland, the Chelmsford surgeon, spoke of the awful wound in William Hales' throat from which he extracted a lump of cloth as big as a hen's egg, comprising part of the man's flannel and linen shirts, his neckerchief and no less than 60 shot of two sizes.

A vital piece of evidence was given by Superintendent Raison: 'I found a piece of printed paper — part of the *London Journal*, on the spot where the deceased fell, which I now produce and which had evidently been fired from a gun. A piece of the *London Journal* was also found on James Thorogood; but the two pieces in other respects did not correspond; the paper wadding in James Guiver's and William Thorogood's guns were of a different kind to that found near the body.' William Simpson, the Boreham constable, witnessed that when he had Thomas Thorogood and Ebenezer Chalk in his custody, Chalk said, 'It's a bad job for us — I was there. I wish I stayed at home', but Thomas Thorogood declared 'I wasn't there — I went to bed at ten o'clock last night.'

The constable at Fairstead, Henry Sergeant, described how he went to James Guiver's house at 7 am on that Tuesday and found him in bed, still wearing his breeches and his neckcloth. His coat was laid across the bed and in a pocket was a dead and very wet pheasant. There was also the shot and charge and powder flask that shooting required. So, gradually the evidence against each man present at the shooting was built up. Chalk had made it known that he was prepared to give evidence (hoping to evade subsequent prosecution). After he had been cautioned that the evidence he gave could be used against him he told the whole story:

'On the night of Monday, the 18th, I was at Shadrach's beer-shop in Fairstead, the Thorogoods and Guiver were there also. I had some beer with William Thorogood only; it was about ten o'clock when he left the house; we were all turned out. I stopped in the road; the three Thorogoods started off for home, William staying with me a minute or two then following his brother. Guiver went down the road with me, and went into the house where he lodged; he stopped a few minutes when he comes out with a gun; just before I went home with Guiver, William Thorogood said to me — "We are going for a walk and you can go with us." I said — "I don't think I shall go." He said, "Oh! come on, you won't have anything to do tomorrow; we shall get something before we come back, I dare say." This was before I went to Guiver's; a few minutes after Guiver came out with his gun we happened to be with James, William and Thomas Thorogood in a lane as you go to Lion Hall; they all had guns, single barrelled; I hadn't one. Guiver, when against his door, gave me some shot, which I put in my pocket, but I took no notice of its description; the gun found on my premises does not belong to me.... it has been in its present broken state about a month.' Chalk then described minutely how his comrades were dressed.

He told of how he expressed his reluctance to go along with them, when one of them said, 'Oh! come on!' and James Thorogood echoed that phrase, 'Oh! come on! I won't be taken this night by no-one; I'll shoot any one before I'll be taken this night.' He then described the shooting of the pheasants and how he told the others that someone was coming behind them. They wouldn't listen to him so he told them he was off, and with that ran out of the wood as he heard the keeper shout to his mates. He ran for home as hard as he could, but he saw his mates again at Fuller Street, without James Thorogood, whom they presumed must have been captured.

The earliest photograph of Shire Hall, taken about 1870, where the ill-fated crowd gathered to witness the trial for the murder of William Hales. (Picture: F. Spalding Snr.)

The coroner summed up all the evidence and the jury took no time at all to return the verdict of wilful murder against the Thorogoods and James Guiver. They considered that Chalk had not been present at the scene when the gun was fired. They also expressed their feeling that 'considerable suspicion rested upon James Thorogood as being the man who fired the gun.' The criminal trial had then to be fixed.

This is the point where horror was heaped on horror. On Friday 22nd February the five defendants were taken up the stairs of the Shire Hall, Chelmsford, to the Petty Sessions room where they were to be further examined at noon. Such was the public interest that there was a queue all up the stairs. When the doors were opened to the public there was such a rush that the passageway was blocked and the queue was pushing and shoving on the stairs. The police tried to clear the stairs, they shouted over the hubbub that they were in danger of collapsing, within a few moments that is what happened. The third flight of nine stairs gave way in a crashing, shrieking and screaming which alarmed everybody in the courtroom.

The stairs were made of stone blocks, fixed into the outside wall and resting one on another on the inward side where the balusters were fixed in the step themselves, as they circled round, one flight above another. On each stair of the third flight the crowd was so dense that people were being pressed hard against the balusters. They gave way and then the steps themselves fractured close to the wall. The broken steps and the people on them fell down on to the flight below. This is an eye-witness's view as it happened:

'The scene was most appalling. When those who were uninjured — and in many instances there were most miraculous escapes — had scrambled from the fallen rubbish, the body of one young man was seen lying upon one of the fallen stones, with his face partly cut off, his skull crushed, and his brains scattered about.... It was some time before he could be recognized, but at length he was identified by an inscription upon the watch he had in his pocket as Mr J.E. Moss,

18 years of age, the son of Mr James Moss, builder, of this town. His father at the time of the accident was in the court above, and the deceased was endeavouring to make his way there at the time he thus met instant death. His features were so disfigured by the crushing mass of stone which had fallen upon his head, and his clothes so torn and soiled by the falling rubbish, that Mr Moss, after coming down from the court, stopped to look at the corpse, but failed to recognize it as that of his son....As quickly as possible the other parties were rescued, and taken into the small room between the courts, when Mr Lovell, Mr Copland and Mr Gilson, surgeons, were speedily in attendance....'

Mr Moss's son was the only fatality at the scene, but others were seriously injured and some were given a very poor prognosis. Yet, amazingly, there were hardly more than a dozen seriously injured people out of the 200 to 300 crowded on the staircase. One of the magistrates, Mr A.R. Goodday, was about to climb the stairs when Moss's body fell at his feet and the dead man's blood splashed over him.

Those marooned in the courtroom above, including other magistrates, officials and about a hundred members of the public, had to climb out of a window and use hastily pro-cured ladders to make their way on to the roof of a neighbouring building and so down into the churchyard. But the court had to meet again to deal with that original horror of the death in the moonlight of William Hales. After hearing the last speeches by prosecution and defence the judge summed up, saying, 'The only case therefore, for you to consider is as against James Thorogood; and that question will depend whether you are satisfied that his hand was that by which the shot was fired which killed the man....'

The jury retired for just 15 minutes and then gave their ver-dict that James Thorogood was 'guilty of being an accessory to the murder'. This was sufficient for the judge to put on the black cap and pronounce the sentence of death with a recommendation to mercy. William and Thomas Thorogood and James Guiver were then brought up before the judge and, after pleading guilty to night poaching, and listening to a long and very serious warning as to their future behaviour, they were sentenced to four years penal servitude. No evidence was offered against Ebenezer Chalk and he went free — his reward for turning witness and giving vital evidence.

Life is very strange. Young James Moss might have lived on into the 20th century in Chelmsford, had it not been for another young man in Fairstead who decided to have a bit of fun after a few drinks in a beerhouse. For the sake of stealing a pheasant three men died and others were maimed for life.

The Bells of St Mary's

In 1822 Prittlewell parishioners were wondering who was going to be their new vicar. The man who was leaving, Charles Belli, had been presented to this living by his brother-in-law Dr Howley, Bishop of London and later Archbishop of Canterbury, but he did not stay long. What was it about Prittlewell that made him want to move on? One or two possible reasons may occur to you as we chronicle the experiences of the man who replaced Belli.

He was the Reverend Doctor Frederic Nolan, Irish by birth, a Fellow of Oriel College, highly qualified — but, as Philip Benton says in his *History of the Rochford Hundred*: 'He was a very able linguist and a learned man, and one of the most accomplished, ripe, and masterly scholars in Europe, but alas! for a preacher, he had an impediment in his speech. This was fatal to his usefulness, and he may not have possessed all the attributes necessary for success as a country clergyman.'

Prittlewell was at that time still a country parish, though its 'South End' was being developed as a sea-bathing resort. Its inhabitants by and large were still of old Essex stock with that character of few words, no-nonsense, hard-work-never-hurt-anybody which personified the Essex landworker or fisherman.

The trouble with Dr Nolan was that his interests in the classics and the ancient languages like Chaldee, Syriac and Sanscrit, and in the esoteric study of religion, could not easily be understood by the good, honest folk of the parish church of St Mary. When he came here in 1822, Rev Dr Nolan was in the process of publishing his *A Harmonical Grammar of the Principal Ancient and Modern Languages; viz: the Latin, Greek, Hebrew, Chaldee, Syriac, and Samaritan, the French, Italian,*

Spanish, Portuguese, German and Modern Greek — in two volumes. To most of his parishioners the title itself was a mystery. Despite all the troubles heaped upon him he continued in his scholastic researches, publishing even more abstruse works at three or four year intervals. He had his own printing press installed at the vicarage so that he could be on hand to supervise closely the work of the compositor and the printer he employed at his own cost to produce his works.

Another difficulty for Dr Nolan was that this was the first time he was actually in charge of a parish, with a curate to assist him. He had been ordained in 1806, took priest's orders in October 1809 and then served as a curate at Woodford, Hackney and a City parish, St Benet Finck, before being presented to Prittlewell. The high quality of his literary and religious research brought him membership of the Royal Society of Literature in 1828, Fellowship of the Royal Society in 1832, and Honorary Membership of the Statistical Society of Paris — but it did not win him many friends in the parish.

It was the bells which were to blame for the fiasco that followed. Prittlewell had a fine peal of six bells and the bell-ringers had gained a great reputation. An entry in the church records of 1788 lists the days on which the bells would ring — 29th May, 4th June, 5th November and Christmas Day. The ringers thus ordered to perform were paid ten shillings between them, and no doubt at the end of it all they refreshed themselves from one of those great jars of ale specially kept in belfries for the purpose. Of course there were days of practice as well, for these ringers wanted to give their best on the great occasions. There were other days of the year when they all got together in the belfry. New Year's Day was cheerfully welcomed in, Fair Day was announced with official clangour, and then there were those irregular days of joy and celebration such as Coronations or triumph of arms by sea and land. It should be noted here that the law of the church requires the consent of the priest to any ringing of the bells, conversely they cannot be rung without the churchwardens' agreement. You can imagine the noise occasioned by these

The church of St Mary, Prittlewell, built in the Perpendicular style, boasted a fine peal of six bells and a team of relentless bellringers.

bells, the disturbance they would cause to anybody living in the neighbourhood of the belfry. The person who lived nearest the church tower was the Reverend Doctor Nolan! When he came to the vicarage he agreed to the campanologists' rules, one of them being that ringing could begin at five o'clock in the morning. He did not realise what he was letting himself in for.

Yet Dr Nolan did his best to fit in with the old parish practices. When the dire significance of that ringing regulation came home to the vicar and his wife he asked the bellringers if they would kindly delay the start until 8 am. The ringers refused what seems, in retrospect, to have been a very reasonable request. For 18 years the poor man and his wife suffered this aural assault. Philip Benton, sympathetically summing up the situation, quotes the old verse:

'Disturbers of the human race,
Your bells are always ringing,
I wish your ropes were round your necks,
And you upon them swinging.'

One sunny, summer Sunday, it was 14th June, 1840, the bells had been ringing for hours. By half past nine it became just too much. Something snapped in Dr Nolan's brain. He seized a carving knife from the kitchen, rushed across to the church and bounded up the belfry stairs. The bellringers would not have been surprised to see their vicar; he had protested many times — but to see him tousled, red-faced, out of breath, and waving a carving knife, well, that was a new and terrifying experience. The vicar, shouting his annoyance and whirling the carving knife above his head like a dervish, tried to slash the bellropes.

Some brave soul among the ringers restrained him and, as he realised at that moment the ignominy of his position, he retired discomfited, defeated. It certainly stopped the bells that day, but the matter did not end there; the bellringers took out a summons against the vicar and he issued a cross summons. Both parties were told to be of good behaviour, but that could not stop the vendetta. Doctor Nolan stopped the ringing most effectively by locking the church door and having it guarded by the police.

That made the ringers really wild, they and their supporters stoned the vicarage, breaking windows and shouting abuse. Dr Nolan and his wife, fearing serious physical assault, armed themselves with pistols. As the stoning continued on successive nights the defenders of the vicarage fired their pistols to frighten the agitators away. The ringers tried another tack. They found that by climbing ladders on to the roof of the church they could get into the belfry by another door. Once

Feelings ran high in Prittlewell village, when an effigy of the Rev Dr Nolan was publicly burned on Guy Fawkes Night.

again the noise of battle was heard as shots rang out from the vicarage in a confused struggle between the pro-bells and the anti-bells. Some say that groaning was heard as if someone was shot, but it was all hushed up, for no-one wanted the police to start wholesale arrests.

Dr Nolan's next step was to report the ringers to the ecclesiastical court which, in those days, still had power and influence. Five ringers were named as defendants. Their supporters showed their fury by the public burning of an effigy of Dr Nolan on Guy Fawkes Night. Many a jeering sobriquet was shouted in the streets, and whole poems were composed and published for the delight of the public and the vilification of the vicar. The words of one such poem have survived; too long to quote in its entirety, but this is the gist of it, sung, it is said, to the tune of *The Mistletoe Bough*.

The Village had long been quiet and still,
The Parson had always enjoyed his will,
And all his Parishioners feared his frown,
Looking with awe as he pass'd through the Town.
The Children all curtesied or made a bow,
As every Child to a Parson knows how.
Angelina looked bold as she gazed around,
Triumphantly striding in haste o'er the ground.
      But Oh, poor Freddy is done, Oh.
This had long been the case, and 'tis known by us all,
Each day as they strutted to Middleton Hall.
But time alters all things, and so it has here,
Although the poor Doctor himself thinks it's queer;
For whenever he strutts or parades through the place,
He is hooted and hissed by each child to his face,
Though a bludgeon he carries, the young brats to chastise,
They still will continue increasing their cries.
      But Oh, poor Freddy is done, Oh.
Now the cause is quite clear, tho' the Doctor can't see,
And yet it has long been detected by me.
The Sermons he preaches are threadbare and stale:
Tho' attentive you listen to hear him you fail.
Then his brogue, tho' not Irish, none can understand,
Although he's a native of dear Paddy Land;
And should a Friend die, or your Father, or Son,
You must have been buried exactly at one.
      But Oh, poor Freddy is done, Oh.
Now the Church is deserted, and the Pews nearly bare,
Yet however unwilling, ('tis truth I declare),
The Bells shall not ring, and no Church Rate shall be,
Until from the prison James Beeson is free.
Since this is determined, and must be our plan,
When a Meeting is called pray all come to a man;
Be firm, stick to this, and the means may not fail,
For why should a Ringer be shut up in Gaol?
But Oh, poor Freddy is done, Oh.

The Angelina mentioned in this poem was Dr Nolan's wife. The five ringers had ignored the summons to attend the court and so incurred fines for contempt. When they were not paid one of the ringers, perhaps we should call him the ringleader, James Beeson, was taken on a Sheriff's warrant and lodged in the Chelmsford prison. For 13 weeks he lay there, until a public subscription in Prittlewell raised a sufficient sum to secure his freedom, after he had sworn on the Bible that neither he nor his companions in campanology would revile or molest the vicar again.

That solution to the storm in a belfry seems to have worked, for Dr Nolan stayed on at Prittlewell for another 24 years. He died in Ireland and was buried there, at Navan. For many years he had left church matters to his curate while he travelled extensively and continued his researches. A footnote to a history of the church at Prittlewell shall be his epitaph: 'Surely this man was misunderstood in Prittlewell'.

The Battle Of Tilbury

Where did the name for that very English game of cricket come from? Historians are puzzled, etymologists compiling their dictionaries declare its origin is unknown, but *Chambers's Encyclopaedia* is more positive. It favours Professor Skeat's theory that it derives from the French 'crice' — a staff. Games with a staff, or stick, and ball had been played in England for 300 years before 'crickett' finds its first mention in the records of the Borough of Guildford for 1597.

It was a man of Essex who was one of the first to explain the intricacies of the sport. Joseph Strutt was born in 1749 at Woodham Walter and went to Chelmsford grammar school. After an apprenticeship in art he went on to write, illustrate and engrave several large and beautiful books on a wide range of subjects from *The Regal and Ecclesiastical Antiquities of England* in 1773 to *The Sports and Pastimes of the People of England* in 1801. Under 'Cricket' he writes, 'The exact origin of cricket is somewhat difficult to determine, but there is no doubt whatever that it is a game essentially and exclusively English in its rise and development.' He traces the origin of the game back to 1300 at least through a mention in the accounts of King Edward I. A manuscript of 1344 in the Bodleian Library has a picture of a woman throwing a ball to a man with his bat raised to strike it. However, for all the manuscripts he studied he could not find that vital symbol of modern cricket, the wicket.

Mention of the game by its modern name can be found in one of Lord Chesterfield's famous 'Letters to his Son' of 1740, where he says, '.... if you have a right ambition you will desire to excell all boys of your age at cricket.' The wicket gets a very

A print showing Tilbury Fort in December 1818. First built in 1539 to guard the approach to London up the Thames, the fort had settled into a slow decline in 1776 when it was chosen as the stage for the momentous cricket match.

definite mention in a poem published in the *Gentleman's Magazine* for 1756 which ends:

> 'Yes, all in public and in private strive
> To keep the ball of action still alive;
> And just to all, when each his ground has run,
> Death tips the wicket, and the game is done.'

So the game was thriving by the middle of the 18th century and in Essex there were keen adherents of cricket.

Thus the stage was set for just another cricket match — but one which turned out to be the most violent confrontation in the history of the game.

From a 14th century manuscript, this drawing shows a woman in the act of throwing a ball to a man who elevates his bat prior to delivering a back hand stroke.

It was a widely advertised event. An eleven representative of Essex was to meet a specially selected Kent side on 29th October 1776 on the green in the very shadow of Tilbury Fort. The Kent side proposed to row across from Gravesend. Since the fort plays a major part in the drama which followed we should sketch out its story. It was first built in 1539 to guard the approach to London up the Thames. The entire complement consisted of eight men under the command of Captain Francis Grant who received a shilling a day for such responsibility.

The fort and its men were appreciated or neglected according to the military climate of the times, like Kipling's 'Tommy':

'It's Tommy this, an' Tommy that, an' 'Chuck him out, the brute!'
But it's 'Saviour of 'is country' when the guns begin to shoot.'

So all down the years the fort would sink into rack and ruin, only to be hurriedly rebuilt and armed whenever risk of attack by some foreign power threatened London's safety.

52

This drawing, dating from 1270, shows a game which appears to be a possible forerunner but still lacks the vital symbol of modern cricket, the wicket.

Daniel Defoe, writing of his tour of the whole country in 1724, spoke of the 100 powerful guns mounted here. In the middle of Victoria's reign a big overhaul was put in hand. Then it again crumbled into obsolescence, was decommissioned and finally passed into the care of volunteers who have worked hard to bring it into a state of interest to the modern visiting public.

To set the scene in 1776, imagine the fort settling slowly into decline. Its big parade ground was weed-grown and its barracks were largely empty. The place was on a repair and maintenance footing with a small complement of men including a number of soldiers convalescing from wounds and illnesses. Some of them would be off duty that afternoon and looking forward to the match — the highlight of the day in what was then a rather remote and inactive military station where nothing ever happened. They could not have imagined the scenes which were to follow so swiftly.

The Men of Kent and their supporters were seen approaching in their boats. They came ashore at the landing stage in an excited little group and the Essex captain and his men went forward to meet them. All was set then for the great match. But wait a moment! An Essex man espied among those men of

Kent a player who was not qualified to represent that county. Demon bowler or mighty batsman, we do not know what he was, but even in those days there was trickery in cricket and the Kent team was prepared to go to great lengths to gain victory over their neighbours. Smuggling in a star player from another county and giving him a sovereign or so for his pains and his valuable runs was a great idea — if you could get away with it.

The Essex men saw it in a very different light and, after a lot of arguing and shouting by most of the men on both sides, they refused to play unless that impostor was dropped. Tempers frayed, fists were raised, and blood flowed. Truly it became a running battle, the like of which even the hardened soldiers had not seen. Kent was getting the worst of it when one of their number, maddened with rage, ran into the guard-house across the drawbridge of the fort. He wrenched the musket from one of the invalid soldiers on guard duty that day, dashed back out with it and, firing at one of the Essex team, dropped him dead on the pitch.

The noise of the gun stopped everyone in their tracks for a split second, then the roaring noise of battle burst out with renewed ferocity. Both teams rushed to the guardhouse and grabbed what weapons they could. It is something of a relief that in those days a musket could only be fired once before a complicated reloading of powder and bullet was required. Even so a great deal of damage was done. In the absence of the officer of the guard the sergeant had only four men under his command at that moment. It was impossible for them to quell the riot, or to prevent the cricketers from commandeering their guns. In a few minutes of sheer bedlam the sergeant was shot dead, an old, sick soldier was bayoneted in the stomach and many other bullets and blows were exchanged before the realisation of just what they were doing dawned on the Essex players. Rallied by their captain they pulled out of the fight, dashed across the drawbridge and scattered in all directions. The Kent side made for the landing stage and pulled away across the Thames as fast as they could.

And they call it sport! From the newspapers and the Quarter Sessions records now existing it cannot be confirmed that these cantankerous county cricketers were ever caught or punished.

But the game went on. That it was still arousing hostility even at a local level can be seen from a result reported in the *Chelmsford Chronicle* and the letter which followed that report. The paper reported on 25th June 1790: 'Last Monday a deciding match of crickett was played between eleven gentlemen of Boreham, and eleven of Little Baddow, which was won by the latter at one innings,

> Boreham 1st Innings 60
> 2nd Ditto 56
> Little Baddow
> 1st Innings 124'

There was more to this simple scoreline than met the eye, however, and a letter of thundering rebuke and refutation appeared in the next issue:

'Mr PRINTER, SIR, As the Baddow gentlemen thought proper to insert in your last, the state of the game of cricket which Boreham played with them on 21st June, and being in haste and cautious of trouble neglected mentioning the game played the Monday before at Baddow which you will permit me to state as follows:

> Baddow First Innings 20
> Ditto Second 32
> Boreham First Innings 54

Having no occasion for the second by having two runs to spare. The Monday following being fixed for the next game, and it being such an unequal game before, Boreham thought proper to change some of their players, and take in some young lads, in order to make it more equal, and to promote Baddow's interest and secure their credit, as a neighbouring parish; but the lads trifling with them too long, as a cat does with a mouse, thereby made a loss; and at the close of the game some windy bystanders were of the opinion that Baddow could beat Boreham if Boreham played their best; a proposal was made by the Boreham gentlemen, to play with them for *eleven half guineas*, which was refused; and to back their opinion and try their cricketers manhood, there are eleven in Boreham will play the game called cricket, with any eleven residing in the parish of Baddow, for *eleven guineas* against *eleven half guineas*, or what sum they please, and Boreham will play the odds; and if this pill won't digest, apply some other remedy. A PLAYER'

What fierce emotions that gentle sound of leather on willow creates.

The Village Hampden

★

Henry Nunn was born in 1836 and died 10th November 1896. Much of his life was lived in a cottage in Swan-yard off East Street, and at the smithy at the end of the same yard in Coggeshall. He married, and at his death was survived by three sons, five daughters and a granddaughter. The whole town mourned him, he was so popular; he was always called 'Dick' when hailed by one and all as he strolled down the street. The reason for his popularity was his intense interest in his home town of Coggeshall — in its buildings and in its general environment as it concerned his fellow inhabitants. He had a wonderful sense of humour which disarmed opponents, and he was as ready to tell a joke against himself as against officialdom. He wanted everybody to know, however, that his actions on behalf of the community were to be taken as seriously as the spirit which inspired them.

One obituary sums up: 'The deceased was well known as the self-proclaimed champion of the people's rights. It was through him, and by his own hands, that the iron bridge was placed across the stream at Coggeshall, and Dick will also be remembered as having been connected with other events of the neighbourhood from which he did not escape so happily. He was great on the question of footpath preservation through fields; he objected to eyesores in the shape of dilapidated buildings by the road side; and one of his earnest desires was to see Grange Hill, Coggeshall, levelled. He always declared that this hill was dangerous both for man and beast. Nunn's enthusiasm in any matter which interested him was very remarkable.... He certainly had a wonderful experience, and he used to tell of it in the most humorous language.' Another writer said, 'In Dick's opinion the labouring classes laboured under many wrongs, which he set himself to redress.'

Yet Dick did not embark upon his crusade of public protest until he was 50, in 1887. He celebrated Queen Victoria's Golden Jubilee in a most unusual manner. There was an old cottage near the churchyard gate, unoccupied for years, with shaggy, rotting thatch and bulging walls. It was also obstructing the view of the parish church. Dick called it: 'An eyesore and a disgrace to the beautiful and sacred edifice.' So, without reference to the owner, our bold blacksmith turned up one day and began demolishing that cottage.

The news soon got round and a little crowd loitered to see the outcome. A local solicitor warned him that he could find himself in trouble with the law: 'Do you know that this cottage is the property of the lord of the manor?' Dick flashed back: 'A pretty lord of the manor, to have such property as this!' Despite other friendly advice and some very angry argument, Dick kept at it, finished the job, completely demolish-ed the pitiful little cottage and had all the piles of thatch and rubble carted away.

He was hauled up before the Witham magistrates, but the lord of the manor, through the solicitor, withdrew the prosecution and Dick walked out of the court with his character unstained — enhanced in fact. This first protest demonstration pleased him so much that, back in his smithy, he fashioned a plaque of iron and had his inscription painted upon it:

'In Queen Victoria's Jubilee year,
A wretched cottage was standing here;
Pulled down by Henry Nunn, Long may she reign.'

He then had it fixed upon the wall of the adjoining cottage for all the world to see.

Dick's next undertaking in the public interest was in 1892. This was the situation — a bridge over the river Blackwater, connecting two footpaths, had been a real public amenity,

This picture of 'Dick' Nunn (inset), and the bridge that he built, was taken on the day of its opening, 31st August, 1892.

allowing a pleasant cross country walk. In those days, too, it was a very useful short cut for many an agricultural labourer who had to walk miles to work from distant villages. But the bridge had rotted away, fallen into the river and for 17 years that useful route had been closed. There had been representations to the parish authorities, but they were so slow to act in the matter that Dick lost patience. So, 'with an amount of public spirit which is very praiseworthy', Dick announced that he would make the bridge himself. He did, in the yard outside his smithy down Swan-yard. He made an iron bridge, 30 ft long, a single span rising three ft in the centre, with handrails on either side, wide enough for two people to walk abreast. He fitted rather cunning bars to each end so that cattle could be prevented from wandering across the bridge in search of greener pastures.

59

On its first appearance it was painted with pink primer —
a shock to the eye in such a green environment. Dick had paid
for all the materials himself, and had put in a great deal of
time and hard work on the project for which he was not paid.
When he had first mooted the idea, W. Bindon Blood, solicitor
for the riparian landlord, wrote a letter of protest against the
replacement of the bridge. He actually visited the spot when
Dick and his friends were putting it in position, but he made
no further objection. Perhaps he and his client saw that Dick
Nunn's powerful public support made discretion the better
part of valour!

On Monday, 29th August 1892, the iron bridge was lifted on
to two trollies and taken across the fields to the river. The
fixing went very well. It was set in concrete on each bank and
was further supported by iron rods fixed in the river bed. Dick
expressed satisfaction with his handiwork. On the following
Wednesday afternoon several hundred people assembled on
the Market Hill in the centre of Coggeshall to form up in a
procession and march to the river. The Coggeshall Town Band
was there at four o'clock, under the leadership of Mr Thomas
Ely, to head the procession in musical merriment to the house
of local worthy G.F. Beaumont, who had consented to perform the opening ceremony. He and Dick then led the noisy
throng, including many notables of the area, through the town
and out along the Braintree road, over a five-barred gate and
across 'Crops' meadows to the river bank.

Despite a shower of rain everybody was in high spirits, the
band kept up a lively selection of marching music, including
'Ta-ra-ra-boom-de-ay' — 'Every youngster about the place,'
reported the paper, 'was exercising his lungs in rendering his
own particular version of the air.' The mind boggles! The rain
had ceased as they walked the footpath, and soon they had
reached the bridge. Those ingenious cattle bars were released
so that people could gather at both ends, while one old man,
Henry Pudney, got so excited that he danced a jig in the middle of the bridge, at the same time singing an impromptu
ditty in honour of the bridge-building blacksmith.

Then Dick took up his position on the highest point of the bridge. In his usual effervescent style he said this was the largest number of people he had ever had listening to him but he hoped it would not be long before he had an even bigger audience. 'You don't know what's coming for the future', Dick warned, which caused some laughter and a lot of cries of 'Hear Hear!' from the crowd, for they all loved Dick as the champion of their local rights.

Dick explained that he had shown Dr Simpson a copy of the *Essex Newsman* which showed how Tillingham had fought for a similar bridge. The doctor had urged him to take the matter up for Coggeshall and he had replied, 'I will, sir, I'll throw a bridge over the river!' and the doctor replied, 'If you will I'll give you a sovereign to start.' That was how it began. Some people had laughed at him, said he was an old fool, but, now, he had made the bridge which would bear people as thick as bees — who could laugh at him now? He went on that he had been sorry for the poor labourers who had had to walk hundreds of miles in order to get home because there was no bridge there, but now he had put a pass there that would carry them over safely, and it was for them to say whether he deserved credit or not. He hoped everybody would give something towards the cost. He then called Mr Beaumont to open the bridge and yielded his place to much cheering.

Mr Beaumont spoke of the many people from Kelvedon and Coggeshall who had come to honour their friend Mr Nunn. For two months he had worked hard to make the bridge, which connected a footpath so ancient that no-one knew of its first formation. Some people in the crowd shouted their agreement when he said that there were people who had walked that path 60 or 70 years ago — so now they were asserting their right. Owners of property did not like these paths, but the public must be considered, and if they had the right, let them assert it to the bitter end. They could have taken the Coggeshall parish surveyors to court to get the old bridge replaced, but what time and expense that would have taken! Fortunately they had among them a man who was willing to do the work, and he had done it at his own expense. He hoped that everybody would give to a fund which should not only pay for the cost of the bridge but also give Mr Nunn a bonus — he surely deserved it. He called for three cheers for their benefactor and rousing cheers they were.

Mr Brown, proposing a vote of thanks, said he thought the unmarried people in the parish owed a special debt of gratitude to Mr Nunn, because in the old days many a courting couple had plighted their troth when they could wander over the bridge and across the meadows. Now the bridge was back young couples could follow in their footsteps. Mr Beaumont then formally declared the bridge open, adding that it should be called 'Nunn's Bridge' forever. Then everybody crossed the bridge, all 703 of them, and placed in the box held out to them a total of £4 15s 5½d. The procession formed up again, the band struck up, and off they all went, across Curd Hall meadows to the lane to Grange Hill, then through Swan-yard to Market Hill, where, after a final burst from the band, they all dispersed. That bridge still spans the river. Its last complete overhaul was finished on 2nd November 1984.

In just a year Dick was championing another cause. He had a love of horses and could not bear to see them abused in the service of man. He had to watch helplessly as many a poor beast was flogged mercilessly to make it draw its heavy burden up Grange Hill. He wrote to the papers, he pestered the authorities, but he could not get anything done about it — so he decided to find a solution himself. His idea was not to prosecute the waggoners, it was much more basic; he thought to reduce the incline of the hill! So, on Monday 21st August 1893, he sallied forth with four men he had hired to help him and, armed with pickaxes and shovels, they proceeded, if you please, to remove one half of the width of the road. A crowd quickly gathered to watch old Dick and to lend its support. An aged labourer told the story of the operation. First Dick carefully marked out the plan of his work, then his men went at it, they took off the hard rolled surface and then Dick bribed boys with a water cart to fetch water from the river at the

Grange Hill in 1915, showing the men of the Warwickshire Regiment toiling up the hill which so exasperated 'Dick' Nunn.

bottom of the hill. They poured it on the exposed foundations of the road, to soften them, and shovelled away, Dick giving a hand and sweating like a bull. They had thoroughly disturbed 15 yards of half the highway before they could be halted.

What a flutter it caused in the dovecotes of officialdom! Acting Sergeant Mills of the Coggeshall police station telegraphed the county road surveyor and he telegraphed his district surveyor and he gathered his men together and they all descended on old Dick, who, with the crowd on his side, dared them to lay a finger upon him. After a proper battle of words Dick and his little army were forced to retreat in the face of the stormtroopers of the county council and their steam roller. By the time a reporter could get there the excavation had been filled in, regravelled and thoroughly rolled in.

Yet the reporter was able to get a wonderful story of Dick in action again. It was not on the road this time, but on the roof of a cottage, part of Grange Farm just across the bridge from town. 'I joined in the rush that was being made to the spot. There sure enough, through the cloud of dust he was raising, I perceived the demolisher, stripped of his shirt, sitting astride the ridge of the thatched roof, and tearing away at the timber and straw with a vengeance. His face was nearly as black as his anvil, and his "large and sinewy hands" were of the same colour, while the perspiration coursed about his face and arms in rivulets, giving him a most grotesque appearance. He was shouting down to the crowd below, but the only words that reached me were to the effect that it was "a werry dry job", that he "would like a drop o' ale", and that he meant to "finish the jolly lot." Nunn had a formidable-looking tool by his side, which someone informed me was a "4-tined crome", and with that instrument he had assisted himself in crawling up the somewhat steep roof. He also occasionally employed the crome in loosening the thatch and beating it down to the ground. A large crowd had now collected, and the proceedings were regarded by the majority as highly amusing.'

There were some people, like the Congregational minister, Acting Sergeant Mills, and Constables Pittock and White, who endeavoured more seriously and sternly to get Dick to stop. He would not, he defied them all. Farmer Seabrook was brought to the scene by the police. 'Hoy, Nunn,' he shouted, 'what business have you there to do that?' There was an exchange of words. Dick refused to stop, saying, 'I shan't let 'em stand, I have forewarned you about 'em. Do you come up here and try to take me; you try it on, that's all.' He worked away. By this time he had pulled more than a cart load of thatch. 'I shall finish the job. I told you I was agreeable to pay all damages you know. Come down? I should think not. I wouldn't come down if anybody was to give me *fifty* pound!'

Warned there was a wasps' nest in the thatch Dick cried 'Wasps' nest be damned! I hold the fort. No wasps'll ever

One of the cottages in Colne Road attacked by 'Dick' Nunn, who could be seen, 'stripped of his shirt, sitting astride the ridge of the thatched roof, and tearing away at the timber and straw with a vengeance.'

sting me. I'm boss of the show. Oh no, I shan't come down. If I had been lord of the manor I'd have kept these cottages in repair, and let them be for almhouses. But I forewarned them.' Poor Sergeant Mills did his best to get Dick to come down, but in the end, after a great deal of aggravation from Dick's retorts, which caused no little amusement in the crowd, Constable Pittock was ordered to advance with a ladder to the back of the cottage where the thatch swept down almost to the ground. He got up to Dick, and after several efforts in vain he managed to get hold of him by the leg and drag him off the ridge so that both men slid all the way down the thatch, with Dick being caught neatly by the Sergeant and helped to the ground.

He was then taken away in a trap, receiving the homage

of villagers who had heard of the day's doings and came to their doors to give him a wave and a cheer. Though he spent a week in Chelmsford prison rather than find securities for bail, it all ended like every storm in a teacup with both sides giving ground. Damages were put at small amounts, and Dick paid them, partly, I suspect, through public collections! He was bound over to be of good behaviour and so he was, until his death in November, 1896 at the age of 60 years. The *Essex County Standard* can have the last word:

'Dick Nunn, the "Village Hampden" of Coggeshall, has passed away.... The bold deeds of the "reforming" black-smith.... and the memory of his quixotic career will long survive. The principal grievance which fretted his heroic soul was the existence of dilapidated cottages, and more than once before the days of parish councils he would take the law into his own hands and demolish or attempt to demolish the property of others if it offended his own sense of the fitness of things. For his over-zeal in this respect he fearlessly faced the officers of the law, relying upon his strong conviction of the justice and righteousness of his high-handed actions. In some cases his reforming work, though unauthorised legally, proved a genuine public boon in the long run, and his iron foot bridge over the Blackwater, constructed in defiance of the lord of the manor, is perhaps the most satisfactory memorial of all his exploits. He is undoubtedly one of those characters of whom it may be said that the maxim of Mark Antony will be inversely true — the good that he has done *will* live after him. He will be long honoured as an eccentric yet unselfish and intrepid Essex worthy.'

The Daring Aeronauts

★

'A prompt and determined man, most quiet and inoffensive but full of courage, and ready to go anywhere or do anything, not only by sea or land, but in the air also.' That was how the Duke of Beaufort described the author when writing the preface to the memoirs of Sir Claude Champion de Crespigny, issued in a second edition in 1896. Nearly a sixth of this book is devoted to the 'fascinating pursuit' of ballooning which he had taken up in 1882, shortly afer he had settled at Champion Lodge, Ulting. He writes:

'Every person who ventures off solid earth must be prepared to hear of himself being described as a madman.' Universal air travel today has taken the edge off that remark, but in his time, before the Wright brothers' aeroplane made travel by balloon nothing more than a sport, this was the attitude taken towards such intrepid adventurers. Sir Claude sums up the case for the balloonist: '... if some of the least adventurous people could only realise the unspeakable splendour which so swiftly opens out to the gaze of the aerial traveller, they would admit that ballooning has great and natural attractions. The sensations the aeronaut experiences in the ascent, during his voyage through the skies, are pleasurable beyond description ...'

The risk of accidents was shrugged off by the aeronauts but there were some very bad ones. Sir Claude himself was involved in one despite being in the company of the famous balloonist Joseph Simmons who had already made nearly 500 ascents over a period of some 25 years. Having heard of Colonel Burnaby's successful crossing of the Channel, and General Brine's failure and subsequent ducking in the North Sea, Sir Claude was raring to get aloft and try his luck. He did not wish to go to the great expense of buying his own balloon and all the gear associated with it so he enlisted the help of Mr Simmons, engaging him to turn up with his balloon on 10th June 1882.

It had to be at Maldon because there was a gas works there — and in a field right next to it they ran a piped supply and started inflating the balloon. It seemed to take such a long time. Afterwards Sir Claude discovered that the field was owned by the gas company and the manager of the gas works was charging spectators sixpence each to file through the gas works into the field and witness the preparations and the take-off — the longer the inflation took the more sixpences he could collect. What should have taken an hour lasted all morning and by then the wind had got up to such a bluster that Joseph Simmons advised against attempting an ascent. But Sir Claude had become so excited that he would not be deterred. So, about half an hour after noon, Simmons got into the 'car' or basket and Sir Claude climbed in after him, with his family at the forefront of the crowd to see him off. Satisfied with the arrangement of the ballast, Simmons shouted to the men holding the balloon to let go the ropes.

They held on just a second too long, a great gust of wind caught the balloon and the 'car' was dragged all across the field, banging and bumping until it cannoned into a brick wall, with the men still trying to control it with the ropes. Sir Claude took in the situation in a flash, saw that unless the basket could be fended off they could both be crushed, so he got astride the basket and extended his left leg ready to push off. The strength of the wind and the sheer weight of the basket with the two men in it were far too strong for him — his leg was crushed between the basket and bobbing balloon. One of the men who were still hanging on to the ropes was caught between the basket and the wall and had two of his ribs broken.

In all the noise and confusion Sir Claude was hauled out backwards and laid on the ground. Simmons had also taken a nasty blow, saying later that his side 'seemed to be caved in',

This contemporary print shows the scene of the balloon accident at Ulting.

but, thinking quickly he called for more ballast, to compensate for his injured companion, and, in a moment of calm, had the ropes loosed and quickly shot up through the dense, racing clouds. It took just twelve minutes to cross the Channel and by the time he had brought the balloon safely down at Arras the aeronaut had travelled a remarkable 170 miles in under two hours.

The Times commented on the foolhardiness of the major players in this drama which led to such injuries. The newspapers proved all too sadly to be right in their prophecies of further accidents in this dangerous sport, for Essex was the scene of a much more tragic accident six years later. By a strange coincidence it again concerned Joseph Simmons and took place within a stone's throw of Sir Claude's house at Ulting.

On the afternoon of Monday 27th August 1888 Joseph

Simmons, described in advertisements as 'the well-known aeronaut', was making ready his huge balloon *Cosmo* for an ascent from the grounds of Olympia in London. Crowds of people flocked to see him and his passengers, Mr W.L. Field of New Brighton and a Mr Miers, one of the staff of what was then called South Kensington Natural History Museum. The balloon could easily have carried up to a dozen people, but the *Essex County Chronicle* reckoned that Mr Simmons' lack of success in previous projects had rather deterred volunteers from coming forward. This certainly was a big event; Simmons had a hundred soldiers to man the ropes and move the sand-bags used for ballast to and fro until trim and weight were to his satisfaction. The 'car' was no more than an iron basket, affording great strength in the hazards of landing but looking like a huge bird cage without a top. The passengers were made comfortable on a pile of the sandbags and then a small cargo of warm coats, a change of clothing, maps and instruments was taken aboard, together with those essential cork jackets in case of an emergency landing in the sea.

Joseph Simmons was aiming for a long-distance flight, all the way to Vienna, a very ambitious undertaking, particularly as the afternoon was wearing away. He was anxious now to get aloft, shouted his orders, another bag of ballast, a personal carpet bag, at last everything was right. At his signal the soldiers slipped the ropes and the balloon leapt up into a clear sky where the south-westerly wind blew it across London into Essex, staying in sight of the handkerchief-fluttering crowd for 20 minutes.

At a height of around 3,500 feet the *Cosmo* found a good breeze which almost exactly followed the course of the Great Eastern Railway as it reached out to Romford, Brentwood, Chelmsford and Witham. The passengers were impressed by the ease and silence of the journey and by the superb views they were afforded of the Essex countryside viewed from the vault of heaven. Pressure on their ears made them conscious of their altitude, but they were not so high as to experience more than a slight fall of temperature, so they really could enjoy the untrammelled pleasure as privileged passengers on a balloon expedition. For just over an hour they sailed the sky over Essex, covering some 37 miles from Olympia and now they could see the wide waters of the Blackwater estuary stretching away to the east. Mr Simmons suggested that they should take this last chance of anchoring in England for the night. Henry Miers and Horace Field could hardly argue with the expert aeronaut, so they agreed, and stood by to play their parts in the landing procedure.

They had left the course of the railway at Witham on their left and were drifting over Ulting while Simmons examined the landscape below very carefully. Twice they descended by releasing gas, only to find trees and other obstacles blocking a possible landing site so that they had to heave sandbags of ballast overboard to gain height again. It was a time of brisk action and not a little confusion when Simmons saw a field of cut wheat which seemed clear enough for a good landing. It was in the parish of Ulting and was farmed by the local blacksmith, George Wood. There was a snag — the approach was obstructed by four great elm trees on the verge of the road, but this was a chance which had to be taken. Simmons threw out the grapnel, hoping it would hold, on exactly the same principle as an anchor was used at sea. It was supposed to bite into the earth sufficiently to arrest the balloon and allow a direct descent. It dragged through a field of corn grown by Tom Aldham of New House Farm and never found a hold at all. There was no time to retrieve it and try again, they were almost upon the trees.

The most important thing to do now was to lighten the load to get the balloon to shoot up over the elms. The three men threw out all the sandbags they could and *Cosmo* came up safe and clear — it was the trailing grapnel which caused the accident. Hanging 60 ft or so below the 'car', it caught in one of the trees. Thus the balloon was violently halted in its forward motion, but the momentum caused it to rise and fall like a yo-yo on the end of its string. It hit the ground with sicken-ing force. Mr Simmons cried out to the farm labourers

71

who had come running to the rescue, 'Catch hold of the rope,' but the *Cosmo* was like a raging beast in its violent movement and the rope just could not be grasped. The would-be rescuers could only stand and watch the 'car' crash down on the ground again. Then the balloon soared up again to well over a hundred feet and burst with a frightening explosion. It broke away from the 'car' which then came crashing down with such force that all three aeronauts were rendered unconscious.

Seen through the open iron network of the 'car' an observer said that they looked 'like a lot of birds in a cage' — and dead birds at that, huddled on top of each other on the floor. Fortunately two well known Chelmsford men, Mr F. Whitmore and Mr F. Marriage were passing nearby in a trap and they were able to take charge of the situation. They had the men got out of the 'car' and made as comfortable as possible in the field. It was plain to them that Mr Simmons was very seriously ill. They tried to revive him with brandy in small sips from the only spoon-like receptacle immediately available, a metal spectacle case. A lady then appeared who bathed his head with vinegar and water. But this attention was in vain, he did not regain consciousness, so they removed him as soon as they could to the beerhouse nearby run by Mr Turner and a man was sent on a bicycle at top speed to call out Mr Gutteridge, the well known Maldon surgeon.

It was Mr Field who recovered his senses first. He had a broken thigh and broken bones in the other leg and severe shock and internal pains. Mr Miers was lucky, when he came to shortly afterwards he found that he had escaped with no more injuries than a cut on his forehead, two black eyes, and such shock that he was still visibly shaking. They followed Mr Simmons to the beerhouse while plans were made for their further treatment. When Mr. Gutteridge arrived he decided that these two men should be found lodgings in Maldon so that he could the more easily attend them daily. In the case of Mr Field this was not arranged without some difficulty. He had to be kept flat full length, and as he was six feet four inches tall there was not a horse-drawn vehicle locally which could accommodate him. They had to send for a horse-bus from the King's Head Hotel in Maldon and put boards across its seats, secured with ropes to provide his 'ambulance'.

As to Mr Simmons, the surgeon found he was 'beyond earthly aid.' His skull was fractured and he had sustained severe internal injuries. He could not be moved again. At nine o'clock that night he breathed his last, still in a coma. Let the local paper have the last word.

'The crowd assembled outside the King's Head Hotel on Monday night, waiting for the 'bus, was almost as dense as an election crowd, and much excitement was caused by the news of poor Simmons' death. He was well known in Maldon and everyone spoke with regret of his sad end. When it became known that one of the injured men was to be taken to Silver-street, the narrow thoroughfare speedily became choked and it was not without difficulty that Mr Field was successfully removed. There were too many noisy people volunteering assistance, and it must have been a great relief to him at last to be left alone with his doctor.'

The Opening Of Epping Forest

★

On 6th May 1882, Epping Forest was opened to the public at large by Queen Victoria. She did not exactly *open* the Forest — it was open enough already — all too many trees had been felled in the previous 50 years. All the same, Epping Forest would not have been preserved for us in its green woods and sunlit glades if it had not been for the Corporation of the City of London which paid out no less than £250,000 when England was on the Gold Standard to buy out every other owner. But there is a story far stranger than mere generosity in what we might call the chance preservation of the Forest. Its final decimation and destruction was prevented through the obstinacy and determination of one poor, old man.

The attitude to our woods in Essex was always very indifferent. Wood was something to be used to build houses, make everything from carts to cricket bats, to heat the house and cook the meat through a thousand years. No wonder the great Essex forest dwindled down to the degree that in 1907 the *Victoria History of Essex* reported, 'Essex at the present day must be regarded as a thinly wooded county.' With only 3.15% of its total area then covered by trees, it was more than 2% less than the average for England. It is hard to believe that Hainault Forest was recommended to be preserved 200 years ago because it could provide such good oak for building ships of the line, the old wooden walls of England. It is hard to believe because there is not a tree left of that forest. It was completely demolished in the interest of the expansion of the suburbs of London.

Waltham Forest as a whole, containing Hainault and

Epping, was a wild place 200 years ago, and the Epping enclave had a particularly bad reputation. Dick Turpin, in his heyday as a highwayman at the beginning of the 18th century, helped to establish that reputation. He was born in Hempstead in 1705 where his parents kept the Bell inn, changed later to the Crown and later again re-named Turpin's Tavern. In adult life he was a wastrel who took to assault and robbery to support a swaggering life-style. So he came to Epping Forest where he made a hide-out, a kind of cave in amongst the undergrowth from whence he could sally forth on to the London to Cambridge road and hold up people of substance on horseback and in coaches. He already had a price on his head for capture dead or alive. When one man recognised him, Turpin shot him dead and fled to Yorkshire. But the long arm of the law reached out even there, and set him on the gallows on 17th April 1739.

Turpin was a loner; the Waltham Blacks acted as a gang preying on the same travellers. When they had committed rob-bery with violence on the forest roads they skipped back to the slums of London and laid low for a while. Why were they called *Blacks?* A letter written in 1729 gives a clue. It tells of a man's experiences whilst riding through the forest. His horse threw a shoe and became lame. He pressed on to an alehouse and asked for a room for the night, as evening was drawing on. The alehouse keeper looked nervous when he said he had no room, yet the rider saw no other people in the place. He offered a sum the keeper just could not refuse and, after refreshment, retired to his room. In the darkest hour of the night he was awakened by a commotion below. He opened his door just the merest crack, peered down into the candlelit bar-room and listened while a crowd of desperadoes with wild curses and drunken shouts went through a ritual of obedience to their chief, constantly referred to as *Orronoko, King of the Blacks*. Then he quietly closed the door — and trembled the night away!

Another kind of violence was practiced in some of those remote clearings in the forest. Bare-knuckle boxing was banned in the early years of the 19th century, but still there were fights in places like Epping Forest and Canvey Island, well away from the eyes of the law. Epping was very handy for those London lads who liked a little bet. In June 1806, tucked away in the clearing called Padnall's Corner, pugilists Maddox and Cody stripped to the waist and set to. The *Essex Chronicle* tells us: 'After fighting upwards of half an hour, Cody seemed to have the best of the battle, although he was hit a good deal more than his opponent. The ring was broken, either by accident or design, and the combatants were taken away until a fresh ring was made.... Maddox certainly had the advantage of the delay, and the contest was continued three quarters of an hour longer, when the appearance of a detachment of the 10th Light Dragoons occasioned the ring to be broken again. The Dragoons drew up at some distance from the scene of the action, and a Magistrate entered the ring. With a degree of moderation he addressed some of the 'Amateurs' and informed them that the assemblage must disperse, or he would be obliged to call in the aid of the military to enforce his authority.

'A third ring was formed about half a mile from the spot after the cavalry had retired, and Maddox, who had nearly blinded his opponent, entered it to resume the contest, but Cody declining a renewal, the fight was made a draw of.'

Let us return to the violence practiced against the forest itself. Before one old man took his stand against the wholesale rape of its trees there had been earlier protests by inhabitants of the scattered hamlets in the wood against its further despoliation. As long ago as 1572 some people were trying to prevent the destruction of a little bit of the old forest called Knighton Wood. This is what happened.

Bernard Whetstone, lord of the manor of Woodford was given royal permission to chop down and fence off one quarter of his forest land if the folk who lived on his manor agreed. He was ready to allow them certain rights of collecting firewood over the rest of his land, but they would not agree. They knew that once he got that piece of land cleared, development would take place and more of the forest would be

This mural in the lobby of County Hall, Chelmsford depicts the official opening of Epping Forest by Queen Victoria.

cleared. Whetsone angrily sent men into Knighton Wood to chop it all down oblivious of their representations. He did not reckon with the determination of the women of Woodford; 13 of them, with three men for company, went into the wood and stopped Whetstone's workmen.

When he tried again no less than 300 men from Woodford turned up, broke down the hedge and filled the ditch he had dug around it. They burned that hedge and all the stakes that had been driven in. Again he tried to assert his will over his land — the women went in again, beat the workmen with sticks, and took their axes away from them. Whetstone reported to the court that they wouldn't give the axes back! Those brave women of Woodford saved that little bit of the wide-spreading Waltham Forest, and Knighton Wood survived all the development of the suburbs between Woodford and Buckhurst Hill so that it was at last brought to safety under the Epping Forest Acts in 1930.

The current ownership and proper conservation of Waltham Forest was inquired into by 'Lord Portman's Act' of 1849. Commissioners examined all the rights enjoyed and the claims made over the whole forest so that boundaries could be established and encroachments denied. As a result, that part of it known as Hainault Forest was allowed to be totally cleared and all the deer in it relocated or killed. Local farmers were glad, they considered the deer nothing more than a pestilential nuisance. Farmers and landowners in the Epping part of the forest would have liked to see it cleared in the same way, but it was specifically stated in the Act that '...nothing in this Act contained shall extend to that portion of Waltham Forest usually called Epping Forest.'

Yet, with the connivance of the Commissioners of Woods and Forests, pieces of Epping Forest were being obtained by individuals who were prepared to pay well for the extinguishing of all the old rights over it so they could eventually clear it for development. There was now a growing recognition of the value of this forest close to London as a lung of fresh air and a place of innocent recreation for Londoners, rich and poor alike. For all the good intentions and a petition to the House of Commons, nothing useful was done.

The agitation continued, however, and was crowned with success when influential people supported an address from the House of Commons to Queen Victoria asking for Epping Forest to be preserved as an open space to be enjoyed by the public at large forever. It was pointed out that through the 250 years down to 1850 only 600 acres had been illegally fenced in by landowners greedy to add to their property. From 1851 to 1875, says the Report of the Forest Commissioners, 6,021 acres had been stolen in this way. The crisis came when the lord of the manor of Loughton, Rev J.W. Maitland, rector of the parish, looking for the mountain of money which would rise from speculative builders, fenced in no less than 1,316 acres of the Forest and cut swathes through it for roads which would precede its development.

Now onto the stage comes Thomas Willingale, a poor old labourer who lived in Loughton. He had earned part of his living every winter by cutting wood from the Forest — an ancient right granted to villagers which, but for him, had fallen into desuetude. It allowed the lower branches of trees to be lopped for firewood, and in former times had been a vital source of fuel. Thomas determined to continue exercising his right. He climbed the fences or broke them down to do his lopping and he encouraged his sons and his neighbours to join him so that this ancient right was not lost through neglect. The old tradition in the Loughton district was that at midnight between the 10th and 11th of November (St Martin's Day) the folk all gathered on Staples Hill, did their lopping from midnight for a couple of hours, then celebrated with beer round a bonfire before hauling away their winter store of firewood.

Tom Willingale's breaking of the fences to carry on with his lopping was resented by the owner, who had close connections through wealth and class with members of the bench of magistrates for the area. He took Tom and his friends to court, and, though Tom was let off as an old man, his sons and his nephew were sentenced to fines or imprisonment for trespass. The local paper reported the case in full under the heading 'Forest Rights' on 6th March 1866. The defendants were Alfred and Samuel Willingale and William Higgins. They were charged with damaging trees belonging to J.W. Maitland, lord of the manor, to the extent of one shilling and sixpence each, in the cutting of branches from hornbeam and beech trees. The three men answered that all they took from the trees, was in the process of lopping and they had committed that act simply to defend their right so to do.

The Counsel for Maitland addressed the Bench at length to explain that the lord of the manor had entered into an agreement with all the people who held land upon his manor before he fenced off the area. William Higgins, who was a tenant of a Mr Tree, a freeholder on the manor, declared that he was thus entitled to the old lopping privilege. Then one of the magistrates entered the fray on the side of the lord of the manor. He said he knew that those entitled to compensation had been paid, and to those people who had asked for his advice in the matter he had explained the situation and advised them 'not to get into trouble'. Tree himself had received £30) and

An ancient beech tree in the forest, showing evidence of lopping, the centuries-old right granted to villagers.

that was more than had been agreed with any other freeholder. It rather looked as though Rev Maitland had the right friend there on the Bench. The Chairman summed up; the defendants acted illegally, but since the court only wished to stop this breaking down of fences and the continuation of lopping, they would only fine each man two shillings and sixpence plus eleven shillings between them for damages and costs, or seven days imprisonment. 'The defendants,' it was reported, 'who behaved with considerable levity in court, appeared to treat the matter quite in the light of a joke, and said they would each "do the seven days". They were removed from the bar and locked up.'

They chose imprisonment as their public protest. Handcuffed together, they were taken to Ilford gaol where they were put to hard labour, walking in the treadmill, picking oakum and shifting paving stones. William Higgins caught a chill through the dampness of his cell and was ill right through the summer. It has to be said that Rev Maitland suffered a lot of character assassination in Loughton through that same period. One reason was that in May 1866 he bought several cottages in the parish. In July he gave the tenants notice to quit so that he could replace them in houses new–built on the same sites. One of the tenants was Thomas Willingale. Even though the arrangements were accepted by him in his own handwriting, and only later rejected by him, rumour had it that the lord of the manor was trying to get him out of the parish so that he would be disqualified from continuing an action in Chancery against the lord's felling of all those trees and for the upholding of lopping rights. Knowledgeable friends had helped him in this action.

Tom persisted, was evicted from his cottage, and took his family to a dilapidated wooden place at Golding's Hill lent by a sympathiser. He refused all monetary offers to give up his suit — and died while it was still in progress.

His death and the halting of that Chancery suit galvanised public interest. The great break came when the commoners of the Forest got the ear of the Corporation of London, which was itself owner of tracts of Epping Forest. On 21st August 1871 the Epping Forest Act was passed, to put in process over two years a thorough-going examination of all the owners of land in the Forest and the rights of individuals within its bounds. Just a week before this act became law the Corporation of the City of London began its own campaign. It said it could find the money to buy out all owners from a toll they levied on grain imported into or through the City. Their researchers found that the land called Epping Forest included 3,014 acres of land still standing open and partly afforested, and 3,007 acres which had teen taken over by landowners moving their fences ever outwards.

In 1874 the City obtained an injunction stopping any further stealing of land or any further building upon it. What's more, all fences put up in the 20 years previous to the begin-ning of that suit begun by old Thomas Willingale had to be withdrawn back to their original boundaries. Public and Parliamentary interest backed the City's initiative. A local act was passed in 1878 and the Epping Forest Act followed in 1880. Out of the complicated legislation came the cancellation of all the old royal rights to the animals of the Forest, the posts of the various officials and the special Forest Courts. Queen Victoria was to appoint an overall 'Ranger' and the City Corporation was to appoint 'Conservators' to manage the Forest in all aspects dedicated to the recreation of the public.

The Act did not immediately pay compensation for the loss of Loughton's lopping rights, which had been conceded in effecting 'nationalisation', but later the Corporation paid out £7,000 to Loughton and the parish spent most of it on building the Lopping Hall, a public hall for all kinds of activity which still stands there today. The strange ending to the whole story is that this hall, at its opening, was blessed by Rev John Whitaker Maitland, lord of the manor, rector of the parish, the very man who started all the rumpus by enclosing so much of the forest and trying to deny Thomas Willingale's little bit of lopping!

The Foulness Riot

Come back with me to 1828. A look at the local paper of that year will set the scene: 'The Island of Foulness, it appears, has for some time been the scene of intestine broils; and if we give testimony to one party the island contains *smugglers*, whilst the other party as confidently asserts that *poachers* reside there. In this way a spirit of revenge has been kept up, and but for the strong arm of the law, we might expect to hear of something more serious than the charge in the present indictment, which was for a *riot*, and was preferred by Thomas Bennewith, against Jonathan Ballinger, Bennett Forster, Isaac Everett, Ambrose Ballinger, William Monk, James White and Josiah Downs.' These were all names of old Foulness families.

Where is Foulness? It is that horn-shaped island on the eastern seaboard of Essex, on the south bank of the estuary of the river Crouch, cut off from Paglesham, Barling, Havengore and the Wakerings by the river Roach and the numerous creeks and tributaries which head for the wide estuary of the Thames and the North Sea. Before the days of motor cars and tarmacadam it was an isolated place with a very small population. Even 60 years after the events we are about to describe it was still entered in the guide book as: 'A dreary flat, marshy island; the saltings in winter are much frequented by wild fowl, from which fact the island is said to derive its name.' It was not formed into a parish until 1550 and it was still considered a very isolated place in 1861, when D.W. Coller was writing his *The People's History of Essex*. He said that it was reached by a pathway across the sands which could only be negotiated at low tide. It was called the Broomway because its serpentine track was marked by stakes, with a faggot of twigs tied to the top of each to make it more clearly seen in moonlight. The island is five miles long and two and a half miles broad, and its population was no more than a couple of hundred souls. By 1933 the whole island of Foulness, its lands and its buildings, except for the church, the rectory, the school and the mission hall was in the ownership of the War Department. Down to this day no-one can visit Foulness without a pass, and that pass is not easy to get.

In the early 19th century the name of Bennewith was very well known in this area as that of a family of bareknuckle boxers, or, as the paper says, '....formerly of some importance in the annals of *pugilistic* notoriety'. *'Josh Hudson,* however, it will be in the recollection of some of our readers, a few years since, in a field upon the borders of Rettendon Common, proved *Bennewith,* the champion of Rochford as he was then called, to be a *cock* calculated only to crow upon his *own* dunghill.' This was a rather unkind reference to the bareknuckle battle of 4th April 1820, when these two fought for a purse of no less than 30 guineas. Some 7,000 people turned up to see the grand confrontation, but it only lasted eight and a half minutes — Bennewith was knocked out 'and could not be made sensible to come to in time.'

The Thomas Bennewith of our story was not a boxer, for one very good reason, he had a hand blown off when a gun exploded in his grip. The reporter concluded, '... the pugilistic *title* may therefore again be considered to have reverted to the *female* branch of the family, and Mrs Bennewith, who has for the last 20 years . . . gone by the characteristic name of *"Flanking Charlotte"* appears formed by nature to support the character of her family.' It was the riot now being reported that really brought out that character.

The cause of the trouble was smuggling. On this remote shore it was easy to land goods from France and thus evade the customs payment due. Smuggling was considered almost a local industry, not as regular as fishing, perhaps, but a good deal more profitable, and not to be spoiled by some spiteful villager telling the authorities all about a dark night's delivery. One landing was interrupted by the excise men and the smugglers suspected that Bennewith was the informant. They let him know in no uncertain terms what they were going to do to him. Bold as Bennewith was, he was really frightened by these threats, so he took his complaint to the January Quarter Sessions at Chelmsford in 1828.

All those people we have already mentioned had to find sureties for their good behaviour — to keep the peace towards him. Bennewith was so pleased with this triumph that he did not just return quietly to the island. He bought yards of blue ribbon and had his witnesses and his supporters all draped with it as a symbol of victory when they arrived back on the island. He fixed a big, blue flag high up on his house and right next to it placed a gin cask, draped with black cloth — indicating that he was celebrating the death of smuggling in his parish. Mrs Bennewith was just as brash; she paraded round the hamlet of Courts End, north-east of the church, telling everybody in a very loud voice that her husband was master of the place and that the rest of the residents would be wise to come under his protection.

All weekend the flag flew and the gin cask stayed in mourning — and that was too much for the villagers who were still wild about Bennewith's resort to the courts. They arranged a little demonstration of their feelings — they formed up in a procession to his house. It was led by two men on horseback, then came two asses, probably the very ones they used as pack animals to carry the smuggled goods up the beach and across the island to the nearest road for transport on to London. On this occasion, though, the asses, or 'dickies' as they were then called, bore unusual burdens. One had a crudely stuffed male figure strapped to its back, supposed to be in the likeness of Thomas Bennewith, but with a pair of branching antlers fixed to its head. This tied up with the shouted declaration of one of the ringleaders of the so-called smugglers, 'We are independent of all hornyfied cuckolds!' A cuckold was the term applied to the husband of an adulterous wife. It was a great insult to a man to be called a cuckold and the horns were an additional affront — the smugglers had chosen the most obscene and offensive gesture they could think of. Upon the other 'dickey' sat an effigy of Mrs Bennewith, apparently calculated to offend by its crude carica-ture for it was said at the time that it 'was dressed in a manner to represent Mrs Bennewith. Considerable liberties appeared to have been taken with the female figure.' There followed in the train of these offensive effigies 30 to 40 men, women and children, most of the population of the hamlet of Courts End at that time.

Mrs Bennewith did not react as one might have expected from a woman with the nickname of 'Flanking (ie fighting) Charlotte'. It is possible that she had been enjoying some of that smuggled gin, for she came out of her house, in amongst the procession and shouted and laughed and danced the horn-pipe, then went back indoors and fetched out a stone bottle of wine and, in between sips, offered it all round. There were witnesses in court to say that, far from being frightened, she thoroughly enjoyed the whole proceedings.

The court was told that there was a gun fired; but it was loaded with powder only and fired in fun by Mr White the punt-gunner, who made his living by shooting wild fowl on the marshes. It added a little excitement to the occasion. When the procession returned past his house Bennewith rather ruined his own claim of terrorisation by following it on down to the public house where it had stopped for refreshment. He went in and asked for a pint just to show his defiance. The landlord, anticipating trouble on his premises, refused to serve him.

The churchwarden of the parish, Mr Potten, was there and gave evidence in court as a reliable, God-fearing witness. He said that nobody at all appeared to be frightened and that, as far as he could see, it was 'merely a frolic'. Now, at this court in July 1828, the counsel for the defence got up. He regretted that such a trifling matter should occupy the judges and the jury. He argued that on a point of law the charge of riot was not substantiated: '... there was no terror excited,or anything done to excite terror ... the conduct of the defendants arose from the provocation they had received by the exhibition of the colours and gin cask in mourning, and the in-sulting expressions of Mrs Bennewith which they resented by showing their independence, in doing which they certainly indulged in rather coarse raillery ... But still, however libellous this might be, if the indictment was for a libel — yet it was not riotous, as it was calculated to excite no fear ... and that Mr and Mrs Bennewith themselves were clearly shown to have been under no alarm. That in truth they began the game themselves (when they informed on the smugglers) and should remember the old saying that "they who play at bowls must take rubbers." This was the counsel's version of the proverb 'they who play at bowls must expect to meet with rubbers', the rubber being the final game which decides who will be the winner. He was inferring that since the Bennewiths had started the quarrel they had to put up with the response.

But for all his pleading the jury decided that those noisy, jolly islanders were guilty of starting a riot. The judge, how-ever, made plain his view that it was just a storm in a teacup by fining three of the leaders, including Jonathan Ballinger the Foulness constable, who should have known better, and making them and the rest of the 'rioters' subject to being bound over to keep the peace for a year. He knew they would all have settled down again by then. Foulness settled back to years of peace and quiet, then the War Department brought its guns and bombs to the firing ranges, put in its own approach road, and made the island even more inaccessible.

The Flying Flea

★

It was on 13th April 1936, Bank Holiday Monday, that the Flying Flea hit the Essex headlines. But what is, or was, a Flying Flea? And how did it come to settle in Essex? Let Pierre Mignet introduce us to his father. 'In the 1920s in a country house in the south-west of France lived the son of an old local family. He was not very wealthy, but was gifted with a quick mind, plenty of manual skill, and above all else, imagination. Being the son of an artist, and an artist and aviation enthusiast himself, he could not come to terms with the dire effects of the sudden loss of control experienced in conventional aircraft.

'He carried out extensive research in his own way; research that took him away from the beaten track. In 1933 he test flew his 14th prototype. A new aerodynamic formula had been born.

'The aircraft was the Pou Du Ciel or Flying Flea. The man was Henri Mignet.' Henri was born in 1893 near Saintes in the west of France. Thus he was entering his teens when the first aeroplane race in the world was held in his country. That event appears to have been a great inspiration to this most imaginative young man. Even while still at school he had made his own kite and his own camera — put them together and produced some respectable photographs of the roof of his house. Travel by air became his passionate preoccupation. His work up to and through the Great War was as a radio operator, but every spare moment was spent fiddling with planes and their engines.

By 1920 the result of all his spare-time activity was his very own, hand-built plane designated the HM2. 'Henri Mignet 1' had been a glider, made when he was but 19 years old. HM2 would not leave the ground. Henri sighed deeply, took it apart, added bits and pieces and made it HM3. Time moved on. Mignet got married but his aeroplanes were not inspired to take off. HM6 and HM7 passed from the drawing board to the workshop, but still they failed to fly.

Mignet carried on his bread and butter job in radio operations, and his other great interest, photography, took him into the realms of the new cinematography; but at the back of his mind there ticked all the time that basic urge to get air-borne in his own plane. He started again on a new model — HM8, and as he taxied across the field he saw the ground slip away as he revved the engine. HM8 was airborne! But only for a moment; it went into a spin, luckily from a very low level and crash-landed into a complete wreck, with Mignet miraculously preserved from all but minor injuries.

The fact was he had flown his own aircraft, and he wrote articles in magazines which told of his success with a plane made by an amateur and flown by an amateur. He was bombarded with letters. With such encouragement he went on to write a whole book on his tribulations and his triumphs — including all the working drawings and instructions for building, by the man-in-the-street, of what we today would call a 'microlite'. The book was snapped up, sold out within weeks and a second edition was just as quickly exhausted. The newspapers took up the new craze and, looking for a catchy name for this tiny, personalised aeroplane, came up with the sobriquet, 'The Flying Flea'.

HM10 introduced further refinements, but Henri Mignet still claimed it could be made and assembled in a 13 ft long room — the front room of an ordinary house; though the wings were, in various modifications, a good deal longer than that! Still there were snags! Mignet patiently worked to iron them out. Model followed model down to HM14. The number of Flying Fleas under construction in the spring of 1935 by amateurs using his instructions was put at 500 and a special society for amateur aircraft builders was formed. Mignet toured its branches, enthusing, expounding, explaining. The first official gathering of 'Fleas' was at Orly, before a crowd of some

Mr W. A. Pearce circles the field in his Flying Flea at Canute Air Park, Ashington on 13th April, 1936. The Flying Flea G-ADPX in the foreground, was built by E. G. Perman & Co. and featured a Perman Ford engine.

1,500 people. Each Flea was the individual product of its own builder. Some were more enthusiastic than careful; it cannot be denied that there were a number of accidents with these primitive machines.

The craze spread to England. The *Daily Express* took up the Flying Flea, had Mignet across to tour aero-clubs and show off this amazing Frenchman. And so we come to that Bank Holiday Monday. What a flutter it caused at Ashingdon, just north of the present Southend Airport! On the following Friday a keen young reporter wrote:

'AERIAL THRILLS. A FLYING FLEA ON FIRE.

Several thousands of people, some from a considerable distance, went to the Canute Air Park at Ashingdon on Bank Holiday for the "Flying Flea" rally, the first event of its kind in Great Britain. There were eight "fleas" present, one coming from South Shields, another from Surbiton, and two from

London. A drone and an auto-giro also attended. The drone, a seven horse-power machine [in other words a power-assisted glider], provided the spectators with a thrill. As it was descending black smoke was seen to be coming from the neighbourhood of the cockpit, and when it landed flames burst out. The pilot, Mr Neville, of Forest Gate, got out unscathed. One of the wings of the machine was damaged, but officials with fire extinguishers saved the drone from complete destruction. Later, when the auto-giro was about to take off, the wheel brake locked and the machine overturned, but the pilot, who came from Ford, Sussex, was unhurt.'

The Flying Flea got a further mention on the same page: 'A full programme, arranged by Southend Flying Club, was carried out before a large crowd at Southend Municipal Aerodrome on Bank Holiday. Landing Competitions .... [were held]. A bombing competition, with so many entries it could not be completed, is to be continued next Sunday. Flying Officer G.P. Longfield gave an exhibition of aerobatics, and Mr W.A. Pearce, in a Flying Flea, demonstrated controllability and also flew in formation with the Club machines. Later the Flea made a trip to Ashingdon and back. In all, the machine was up for over two hours.' That was quite a remarkable achievement for a Flying Flea!

In those days Air Commodore A.E. Clouston was a 28 year old test pilot. This is how he saw that day:

'The principle of the Flying Flea, the smallest aircraft ever to fly, was a biplane powered by either a motor-cycle or small ten-horse-power motor-car engine. It had a control stick that moved backwards and forwards, tilting the main wing above the pilot's head up and down for diving and climbing respectively. There was no lateral stability, and the Fleas were always on the verge of stalling. A pilot had to use rudder alone to skid round in a turn.

'Those Fleas that did get airborne never succeeded in flying much higher than the tops of the hedges, and often had to fly through gaps in the trees and below the house-tops. Many people, including some very highly qualified RAF

91

instructors, were losing their lives, but the press and the enthusiasts who had not been killed said it was just poor flying.

'Like most pilots I was very interested in the idea of the Flea, and when the first British Flying Flea display was advertised I flew down with another test pilot, Flight Lieutenant "Fanny" Adams, in my Aeronca. The display was to take place in a large field near Southend. Owners were invited to take along their Fleas, whatever the stage of their construction, and also to make their first test flights from the field that day. A Circus of Fleas would take the air, the advertisement enthusiastically announced.

'We arrived early, but police were already having difficulty in controlling the crowd. Fleas in various stages of construction were being dragged behind motor-cars, and even motor-cycles. Others came on trucks. Out of the dozens that were turning up, only one Flea, in the hands of an expert, flew down to the display...

'The Fleas were parked in a long line on one side of the field so that the public would have an opportunity of viewing the makers' efforts. One enthusiast with a commercial turn of mind offered all comers the opportunity to fly his Flea for a fee of five shillings for ten minutes. "Fanny" and I looked at one another, but when we inspected the Flea closely we saw that the owner had sawn two inches off each propeller-tip to prevent it from taking to the air. Small boys, however, readily paid their five bob, and the Flea was in constant use, racing across the field in every direction. At least they got the thrill of travelling with the seat of their pants almost scraping the ground at 35 miles per hour. If they were lucky enough to hit a bump, they were tossed a couple of feet in the air for 50 yards or so.

'The pilot who had flown down in his Flea took off on time on the programme to demonstrate its flying qualities. When he had finished his show, other Flea owners tried to emulate him. Most of them had not been inside an aeroplane in their lives.

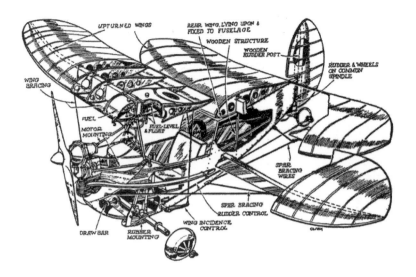

A Flying Flea machine as shown in The Aeroplane Magazine. *By the spring of 1935, the number of Flying Fleas under construction by amateur aircraft builders using Mignet's instructions was put at 500.*

'It was not long before the field was a mass of darting, screaming Fleas trying to get airborne. There was no organisation, control or wind indicator. Each would-be flyer ignored, or was ignorant of, the wind factor, with the result that Fleas were raced across the field in any direction their owners fancied. Fleas crossed one another's paths, missing one another by inches. It was only a matter of time before the inevitable collisions occurred. Fortunately, the damage was restricted to the Fleas, and no one was badly hurt.

'Out of all the attempts, only one Flea at last succeeded in getting airborne. It was flown by a 15-year-old boy, and we discovered it was the five-bob "pilot-yourself" Flea with the sawn-off propeller tips which was not supposed to fly. The lad had run the full length of the field and just as he was about to crash into the hedge, he hit a bump, pulled the stick back, and found himself stuck 15 ft up an old oak tree. He received the loudest applause of the day as he was helped down from the tree.'

Nobody could say that the HM family of planes was a roaring success — in the technical and mechanical sense, but in the enthusiasm Mignet generated, the effort he inspired, the information he provided, he made hundreds of people truly happy, many of them totally fulfilled as they worked away at assembling, modifying and ultimately flying with more or less success, usually the latter, those happily hopping Flying Fleas.

He Wouldn't Pay His Income Tax

He was an honest man, a wealthy man, a man who served his community, but he would not pay his income tax! He was James Samuel Brown, born in Springfield on 7th November 1835, son of James Brown, slate and stone merchant of Coates Wharf at Springfield, the terminus of the Chelmer and Blackwater Navigation.

James was well-educated at private schools before taking his place in the family firm when he was 20 years old. By the time he took over from his father he had become a very able businessman who extended the business considerably and profitably. When he had it set on a successful course, James was able to take part in the public life of the town of Chelmsford. In 1888 he was elected a member of the town's ruling body, the Local Board of Health, just a few months before the town was granted a Royal Charter of Incorporation and became a Borough in its own right. He was straightway elected as a member of the new Borough Council, coming out top of the poll in the South Ward. He proceeded immediately to the status of Alderman, and in November of the following year, 1889, he was unanimously elected Mayor — the second Mayor of the new Borough — which surely says something for his standing in the town. As Mayor he had to welcome the Prince of Wales to the Borough during his visit to the County Agricultural Show.

By this time the business of Brown and Son had moved into steam saw mills, with vast stocks of timber brought in by barges on the canal and trucks on the railway. A survey of Chelmsford's industries in 1891 tells us more: 'The offices of

The first members of the Borough Town Council; Alderman James Samuel Brown can be seen above the mace.

the firm, together with the immense sheds, workshops, engine-room and wharf, cover about two acres of ground. The manufactured goods of the firm consist of all descriptions of wood work required by builders, mouldings for greenhouses, etc, and the facilities provided for the production of large quantities of these goods are such that we have not seen surpassed. Huge stacks of numerous descriptions of timber, chiefly imported from the Baltic coast, are to be seen; while there are also great stocks of building materials of all sorts, for which Messrs Brown experience an extensive demand from contractors and others. Steam power was introduced into the works about 15 years or so back with the most successful results . . . Messrs Brown are also importers of firewood, doing a large business in the bundle trade, supplying shopkeepers and others within a radius of 20 miles of the county town . . . they are in addition engaged in the coal trade, having a depot for this branch at the Chelmsford Goods Station . . . Mr James Samuel Brown . . . is well known throughout the district as a gentleman of influence in the commercial world, in which he holds an eminent place, and is highly esteemed by the whole community.' You cannot develop a business like that without a strong, determined character.

When James Brown received his tax assessment in 1885 he expressed disgust because he was assessed for property tax on the house in which he lived at £2 more than his actual rental. It was not the money, it was the principle of the thing. He tried to see his local Surveyor of Taxes, Mr William Davis, two or three times but was always fobbed off, could only get messages relayed through the Surveyor's clerk to the effect that he must take the usual steps if he wished to plead for a reduction in tax.

That fired him up — he appealed formally against the assessment on his house, and for good measure appealed against the assessment on his business as well. He attended the Shire Hall where the tribunal sat and, much to the Surveyor's discomfiture, he won a reduction on his house tax and was encouraged to further the appeal relating to his business, with the result that he gained a twenty per cent reduction. Triumphantly, but unwisely, he sent a copy of the judgement to 'my friend William Davis' as he put it. He had won the day — but William Davis quietly waited until the time for next year's tax, then assessed our James for Schedule D Income Tax at 36 per cent more. Of course, he said he was not responsible, he was acting on orders from his superiors! He said that if Mr Brown wished to pursue his complaint he must produce for inspection all his business records for the past three years.

What is more, Mr Davis harassed Brown's works manager, Mr Kevan, getting his assessment for income tax raised on the fact that he received an honorarium for playing the organ at chapel on a Sunday. Advised by his employer, Kevan appealed; and had that assessment reduced. How Mr Davis must have ground his teeth! When an inspector came down to look

Mr James Brown was 'well known throughout the district as a gentleman of influence in the commercial world….and [was] highly esteemed by the whole community.' But he wouldn't pay his income tax!

BROWN & SON,

C O A L ,

English & Foreign Timber Merchants,

STEAM SAW MILLS:—

COATES' WHARF, CHELMSFORD,

AND AT

R A I L W A Y D E P Ô T S ,

CHELMSFORD STATION.

A large and well assorted stock of Plank, Deals, and Battens in all dimensions always on hand. Estimates given for quantities sawn to size, and delivered Free within a radius of 12 miles.

SAWING DONE FOR THE TRADE.

Pantiles, Lime, Best Bangor Slates, Laths, Chimney Pots, Drain Pipes, and Sanitary Ware of all descriptions.'

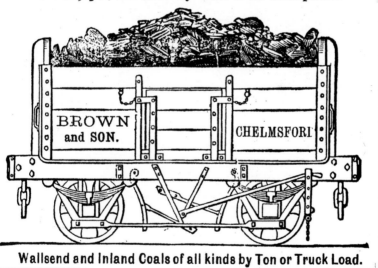

Wallsend and Inland Coals of all kinds by Ton or Truck Load.

*The profitable business of Brown and Son advertising in the **Chelmsford Directory**, 1881*

at these unusual matters in Chelmsford Mr Brown told him, 'as straight as he could' what he knew and thought of Mr William Davis. It ended up with the Board of Commissioners expressing regret that Mr Davis had acted in the way he did. They told him it must not happen again.

The upshot of all the claims and counter-claims was that some tax was still outstanding, Mr Brown would not pay, and the tax gatherers had to get it somehow. So the Tax Collector seized one of Mr Brown's barges, or at least nailed his intention to the mast and advertised it for sale where it lay at the Springfield wharf.

The well known auctioneers G.B. Hilliard and Son were to handle the auction. It was no coincidence that by the day of the sale the barge's name had been altered, in very large letters, to *William Davis*. Mr Brown was not a bit put out — he saw the sale as a chance to make even more public his opinion of tax-gatherers and the complications of the tax itself. So what he did was to invite all his friends and the press to lunch down there on the wharf in a comfortably appointed marquee erected by the local tent and rope makers, T. and C. Godfrey, on the same day as the auction. He saw to it that the area was suitably enlivened; coloured streamers waved out from every available post, a great white ensign floated in the breeze above the entrance to the wharf and below it, exactly at half-mast, there flapped a black flag on which someone had pasted a copy of the handbill which advertised the sale.

Sixty of Mr Brown's friends were pleased to accept this invitation to a lunch which proved to be a very liberal repast, provided by Aaron Mead, landlord of the Golden Fleece. All the best-known tradesmen and businessmen sat down in convivial comradeship. They all had their own battles with the tax man; their sympathy was almost tangible as they ate through eight courses and washed it all down with champagne and wine.

Came the speeches — and Mr Carter said they were there in exceptional circumstances, not only to express their sympathy with Mr Brown in his fight against what he considered

100

was an unjust imposition, but also to protest against the way in which tax was being collected by the man responsible for this town. Everybody enthusiastically responded to the toast he proposed to the health of Mr Brown. Now it was that man's turn to speak. He outlined at some length the tide of trouble which had brought him, and them, at last, to this wharf and the sale of his barge. Mr Pattisson, manager of the Writtle Brewery, backed his friend Brown with an example of his failure to get redress from Mr Davis and his clerks for a humble labourer in his brewery who had suffered, in scale, the same treatment.

Then Ed Durrant got up. He was the local publisher and bookseller, founder of the society much in vogue then called The Odde Volumes, and a whimsical character. He put the feelings on this farrago very neatly: they were there in the first place, to receive the generous hospitality of their friend, Mr Brown, and they would agree that their warmest thanks were due to him for the manner in which he had dispensed that hospitality. Their second object was to enter a protest against the manner in which the income tax was assessed in the county. He hoped that from this meeting some course would be found by which they could put a stop to the inquisitorial levying of the tax. They did not like to have people enquiring into their books. If they paid cheerfully the Board said, 'That district is contented', and gave directions to put up the assessments. Mr Brown had given them an opportunity of protesting in a loyal and courteous manner against the continued raising of the income tax in these depressed times. The time had come when some steps should be taken, and he hoped that a branch of the Anti Income Tax Association would be formed in Chelmsford and that Government servants would show a certain amount of courtesy in the discharge of their duties.

Mr Friend was more forthright, he called the tax assessment scheme a 'system of espionage' and railed against the petty officialdom which 'made it the rule to harass the trading community'. He said that the tax pressed with undue severity upon the middle and professional classes, and it was immoral in that it made them give a return and then declared it to be a false one. How the audience showed their agreement! Several other people spoke in a similiar vein before the Chairman, Mr Brown himself, closed the meeting, asking them to drink a special 'in memoriam' toast, on their feet, in absolute silence, to the health of none other than Mr William Davis, Surveyor of Taxes!

Now the serious business was put in hand at the head of the wharf where the barge *William Davis* was moored. There were flags and bunting everywhere and hundreds of people had flocked to see the outcome of this unusual auction. Mr Hilliard came forward, diplomatically made his excuses for not being present at the luncheon, and called the crowd to order. Mr Brown and his friends boarded the barge, then the auctioneer called for an opening bid. There was a lot of jocularity about this, hiding no little hostility against this unwarranted seizure and sale. Mr Hilliard let them make ridiculous bids, like one penny, saying, 'well, when you have done. I am in no hurry.' Then he asked for reasonable bids. There were not very many. From one shilling the offer rose to £25 and reluctantly on to just £65. There it stayed and the barge was knocked down to that bidder. The tax commissioners thus got £65 out of Mr Brown, but who got that far more valuable barge? It was Mr J.W. Hardy of Maldon. Strangely enough he just happened to be Mr Brown's shipping agent!

The Witham
Railway Disaster

★

It was Friday, 1st September, 1905. Frank Clarke woke up with a surge of excitement. He was taking his family to Cromer for a fortnight's holiday. He was a man with a very good job — private secretary to the Comptroller and Accountant General of the Post Office. It must have been a very demanding position, and a fortnight's recharging of the batteries was a pleasing prospect. Frank, who was 38 years old, had a wife and two children, a girl of seven and a boy of six. They were what you might call the ideal family off on the ideal holiday. They were taking their maid, Maud Bantick, and any amount of luggage and they travelled in from Roehampton to catch the 9.27 am Cromer Express from Liverpool Street. The children were noisily excited, asking endless questions. His wife and the maid fussed over the luggage and getting the family seated on the train. Frank was glad when the whistle went and the mighty steam engine, belching smoke, hauled the 14-coach train out of the station. Now the seaside seemed something more than a dream!

With a rhythmic roar the express rocketed through station after station where London-bound passengers eyed it enviously. It was off to places of pleasure while they were waiting to be whisked off to work. The express rushed on to its first stop at Ilford, then on to Chelmsford by 10.17 am — a very good run on the railway of the day. The engine driver, John Hills, was anxious to get away as soon as possible for he had to keep up a fast run to Colchester. 'Are we nearly there?' the Clarke children asked as the train ran on again at 50 miles an hour.

The wreckage of the 9.27 am fast train from London to Cromer, which left the rails at Witham station, resulting in the deaths of ten people and the injury and maiming of over 40 others.

Let the engine driver take up the story. He had 32 years service with the Great Western Railway, 18½ of them as a driver:

'On Friday, September 1st, I was driving the Cromer express . . . it consisted of 14 carriages, an engine and break vans. I stopped at Ilford and Chelmsford, and all went well until we were approaching Witham station. The signals were all off for me to pass through. I noticed some platelayers at work on the line some distance from the bridge before entering Witham station. They stood in the "up" lines as I ran in. As I entered between the platforms at Witham, I felt a sudden "snatch" on the train, as though an accident had happened. It felt as though the brake had been suddenly applied by the guard in the train. I immediately put my brakes on and shut off the steam and came to a standstill as soon as possible. When I looked behind me I saw that the train, which was all rolling about, had got off the metals. After I passed the middle of the platform the train seemed to become released of some of the carriages. I could not see the carriage which rolled over on to the island platform. Sixty or seventy yards further on I stopped, my engine being still on the metals, and I noticed the "up" train was coming. My mate jumped off the engine to the ballast, and as he did so I noticed the signals for the "up" train were raised. The engine-driver of that train shut off his steam, and we knew then that the train would be stopped. I examined my engine afterwards, and found nothing wrong except the draw bar was broken. I used my engine for the rest of the day...' One of the journeys this driver had to make, though he must have been severely shocked, was to take injured people to Colchester for treatment at the hospital there.

The official statement put out by the Great Eastern Railway three o'clock that same day said, 'The 9.27 am fast train from Liverpool Street to Cromer left the rails at the London end of Witham station, apparently at a crossing, at about 10.30 am. The engine kept to the rails but all the carriages went off. Some of them mounted the down platform. Ten passengers were killed, and about 20 injured. The cause of the accident cannot at present be ascertained.' The number of injured was later found to be very much higher.

Though the platelayers seen by the driver working on the line had another view they could not account for the accident, even though they had been working on the very line on which the express approached the station. Platelayer Arthur Newman told how he was warned to get off the track as the express hove into view. It was such a normal procedure that he did not even look up. When he did, as the result of the noise, all the carriages had left the rails. All he could declare was, 'Nothing I did regarding the work to the sleeper would affect the safety of the train.' His workmate, Maurice Pavelin, backed him up, 'We had loosened the ballast ready for opening the sleeper, when the forman came and we moved aside for the train to pass.'

The most dramatic view, described in a cryptic manner,

105

The sixth carriage mounted the platform and overturned, smashing into matchwood under the weight of the undercarriage, bogeys and wheels.

was that of the clerk in the bookstall, 'I was in my office when I heard the Cromer express coming, and I heard a smashing of glass and breaking of timbers. I rushed out of my office and saw the corridor carriage turning off the metals towards the "up" platform, where it stopped, and other carriages ran across in differing directions, the couplings coming out as the train broke up.' Imagine the full impact of that crash on the people on the platforms. They had stood back from the edge as the express came thundering through, then, to their horror, the coaches broke away and piled up, on and overhanging the "down" platform. The fifth carriage smashed into the porters' rooms there, demolishing them completely in a deafening noise of tearing metal, splintering wood, breaking glass and screaming people. The sixth carriage rushed on in its wake, turned at right angles, fell heavily on its side and rolled over completely with wheels uppermost. The great weight of the undercarriage, bogeys and wheels caused it to collapse like a crushed eggshell. Succeeding coaches crashed into each other with diminishing violence, so that, while the foreparts of the eighth to eleventh coaches were crushed, the buffers of the twelfth to fourteenth coaches absorbed most of the shock though many windows were broken.

One of those strange coincidences so often associated with such tragedies was that these last coaches were carrying a party of 40 children from Dr Barnado's, on their way to holiday at Felixstowe. Every one of them escaped injury —and what a story they had to tell on their return! But this train crash was too awful to be dismissed with a light-hearted remark. Ten people were killed in the dreadful high speed crash, and at least 44 people were injured or suffered severe shock. Tears spring to our eyes when we read one paragraph of the *Essex County Chronicle*: 'The dead, dying and seriously injured were all sadly mutilated, fearful cuts revealing themselves in the heads, faces and bodies, their limbs also being torn and lacerated. Some of the sights, indeed, caused the bravest hearts to momentarily shrink and shudder... Many pathetic incidents occurred. A little girl was picked out of the debris with her scalp badly torn. She called out, "Don't you do that again! Don't you do that again! Don't you hurt my mummy!" It is said that her mother is among the dead.'

What happened to the Clarke family in that split second between happiness and tragedy? They had been pleased to get seats in the third carriage. From happy conversation the scene changed in a flash to consternation. The carriages rose up and dropped like a ship in a storm. Mr Clarke was sitting there one moment, and in the next he had disappeared through the bottom of the carriage while his family was showered with wreckage. Help was soon forthcoming. From the appalling wreckage Mrs Clarke and her son were the first people to be dragged clear. She saw her little girl practically covered by debris and cried out for her rescue. Maud Bantick managed to extricate herself. They were all found to be only slightly injured, but Mrs Clarke fainted away with shock. Rescuers were not looking forward to having to tell her of the death of her husband.

It would seem that he was killed instantly. For an hour rescuers worked with cranes and jacks to get an iron beam off him. The report says that when his body was eventually recovered '... it was found to be crushed, and there was a terrible groove across the chest large enough for a man's forearm to be placed in.' Five of the dead were found in the ruins of this one carriage. Mrs Clarke and her children were looked after at a house in Eastern Crescent, Witham, until her brother and sister could take her to her friend Councillor T.J.D. Cramphorn's house in Chelmsford where she recovered consciousness, though her nerves, it was said, were 'quite unstrung'.

Perhaps the most unfortunate death was that of foreman porter Josiah Doole, who had worked at Witham for 40 years and lived on Chipping Hill with his wife and nine children. The report by a policeman states, 'When I arrived on the scene at 10.40 I saw that the porters' rooms had been demolished. I heard that several people were inside the rooms before the crash came, and had not been seen since. I mounted the bricks and debris, looking round, and heard a moan from beneath my feet. I called several people to help, and after we had removed about three ft of broken brickwork we came upon a man's leg. Removing some more debris, we found a man's head in a coal bucket. He was almost in a kneeling position. We pulled him out and saw that it was the foreman porter. He had terrible wounds to his head, but was alive, and was at once removed to the Corn Exchange on a stretcher, but he died a few minutes after he was placed in the building. He was not conscious when we found him, and never said a word.'

S. Woods, a 17 year old porter, was in one of those rooms demolished, so he could truly give an on-the-spot account: 'I was in the porters' room on the down platform . . . Arthur Chalk, George Adams, and J. Pike, 'fellow' porters of mine were with me. In the next office were Doole and the collectors. We heard the Cromer train approaching, and in a second or two there was a crash and I was knocked off my feet. I got up

The dreadful trian crash, involving children and holiday makers on their way to the seaside, shocked the public and caught their imagination.

spluttering, my mouth was full of dust, but I felt no pain. I know now that I am bruised, but at the time imagined I had been pushed over, and I was astounded to find when the dust cleared that there had been a fearful accident. We afterwards discovered poor Doole dead.'

A Mr Faulkner was in the same coach and compartment as the Clarkes. He described the experience as it mounted the platform and overturned: 'We appeared to be flying through the air, and we must have turned a complete somersault. Our carriage was smashed into matchwood. I attribute my safety to having the presence of mind to fall to the floor. My clothes were torn to ribbons. I think my tall hat saved my head, but I never saw the hat again. I was indeed fortunate to escape as I did.'

There were other stories of coincidence and lucky escape One concerned an injured passenger who was being taken along the street by rescuers looking to lodge him temporarily

This extract from the St John Ambulance Book of 1905 commends members of the Brigade who helped in the grisly task of removing the injured passengers from the wreckage, rendering first aid and assisting doctors on the scene, and carrying the dead to the Corn Exchange at Witham.

in a nearby house. A woman opened her gate to show her willingness to take him in — then she rushed forward and put her arms round him with a great cry. It was her grown-up son — she did not even know that he was on his way to Cromer! A Mr Campbell, with his two children, could speak of a lucky escape: 'I joined the train at Liverpool Street . . . The carriage, however, was rather crowded . . . so I got out and entered the carriage behind. The one I left was completely wrecked. I only sustained a shock. I saw the carriage which caused all the trouble shoot away to the opposite platform. It seemed charged with electricity, and turned completely over. I also saw another carriage spring away and catch fire. The Witham fire brigade appeared on the scene most promptly. Had the cry of fire been raised there is no knowing what would have happened. As it was, the passengers were extraordinarily quiet.'

What caused the accident? After 24 hours of investigation the Company's Chief Engineer declared it was 'absolutely unaccountable'. By the following week the inquest had been held and the jury found '... the deaths were due to an accident in consequence of part of the train becoming derailed at the cross roads near Witham station. We are unable to say that such derailment was due to defective permanent way, or the rolling stock, or both. We find that there was no negligence on the part of the Company's servants. We commend the prompt action of the three signalmen, and also the doctors and nurses and others who assisted after the accident. We wish to express our sympathy with the relatives of the deceased, and our hope that the injured may have a speedy recovery.'

Murder Of
The Purleigh Policeman

★

In the course of duty the policeman faces constant threats to his life even in the carrying out of the meanest, most pointless, crimes. Essex has seen the death of more than one of its policemen in this way. The murder of PC George Gutteridge on 27th September 1927, shot in each eye as he lay dying on the road, filled Essex folk with horror and hit the headlines round the world. But another sickening murder of a policeman in Essex has slipped quietly out of the communal memory, or, one should say, it *had* been forgotten but for a very simple circumstance.

In 1988 a survey of all the graves in Purleigh churchyard, made by the parish council, showed that a good deal of damage to gravestones had occurred over the years, through weather and through vandalism. One stone uprooted and left flat on the grave some 30 years ago had weathered badly in this position. However, with patience the inscription could just be deciphered: 'In memoriam. Sergeant Adam John Eves, Essex Constabulary, who was murdered while in the execution of his duty 15th April 1893, aged 36 years. This tablet is erected by the whole of his brother officers of all ranks as a mark of esteem and regard for his bravery.'

The sight of that stone takes us back a hundred years, to the days when there were but two ways of spreading news — word of mouth and the newspaper. From the excellent local newspaper we learn that on the afternoon of Sunday 16th April, 1893, Herbert Patten, walking home from Hazeleigh Hall to Purleigh, saw a revolting sticky red mess on the edge of the ditch beside the gate from Bellrope meadow. The ditch

112

was five ft deep, draining the field on the other side, with six inches of water in it. Herbert was sure the mess was blood. A look into the ditch proved he was right, there down in the water was the body from which that blood had flown so freely.

Herbert was petrified with shock for a moment. Then, because the body looked lifeless, he ran as fast as he could back to Hazeleigh Hall and gabbled out the news to Mr E.A. Fitch, the owner. One of the men was sent to find Police Inspector Pryke of the Maldon station who was, by coincidence, over at the Hall Farm looking into the forced entry of a granary and the loss of corn. So it was that by four o'clock that Sunday afternoon Pryke and a group of local men were at the edge of the ditch, looking down at the body in policeman's uniform which was recognised at once as Acting Sergeant Eves. They found the corpse was lifeless, stiff and cold — and the reason for that mass of coagulated blood on the edge of the ditch and in it was clearly to be seen. Sergeant Eve's throat was cut from ear to ear. There were also three horrible wounds on his head which indicated that he had been brutally battered into unconsciousness before death. Close to the body, tip-tilted in the water, were three sacks of wheat. Inspector Pryke had found his stolen corn — but at what a price!

It was a harrowing task getting the body out of the ditch, but that was nothing compared with the shock of the sergeant's widow when they took her husband's body home to Purleigh, even though she had been forewarned. As one eyewitness put it, 'The grief of his poor wife on seeing the body of her murdered husband being taken home was very affecting.' Superintendent Halsey now took over and telegraphed the Chief Constable: 'Sergeant Eves murdered at Hazeleigh Saturday night while endeavouring to arrest corn stealers. Body found this afternoon. Frightfully mutilated. Six sacks of corn found close by. No arrest at present.' Two senior officers were sent to Purleigh at ten o'clock that very night and the Deputy Chief Constable was there very early on Monday morning. He found, as the reporter put it, 'The

A policeman at Purleigh admires the result of the restoration of Sergeant Adam Eves' gravestone. (Photo: Essex Chronicle)

114

murder has caused the utmost sensation in the usually very quiet district, where Sergeant Eves was universally respected by the law-abiding inhabitants.'

Urgent enquiries established this scenario: Sergeant Eves was last seen alive at five minutes to ten on Saturday night by Charlie Everett, landlord of the Royal Oak at Hazeleigh, when he called in with a notice about poisoning rooks which he wanted put up in the bar. Then he headed homewards, off duty, back to Bury Farm and the footpath to Hazeleigh Hall which would give him access to the north side of Purleigh — and home. This is where the theft of corn and the murder get tied together in a horrible knot.

Let us go back in time to the scene of the robbery. On that fateful Saturday, the 15th of April, John Moss, bailiff at Hazeleigh Hall Farm, had set his men to threshing wheat on the granary floor. There the grain was left in a great mound. On Sunday morning when the bailiff and his wife had gone off to church at Woodham Mortimer, their son Joseph, walking round the farm, found the granary door ajar, with the lock broken, and it seemed to him that the heap of grain was much smaller. Being a Sunday morning, with so many people at church, it was not easy to get help. Eventually the farmer, Mr E.A. Fitch, who employed Joseph's father, sent the young man to Inspector Pryke at Maldon. In those days, when horses and bicycles were the quickest form of personal transport these journeys by all the parties took some time and it was gone noon before the inspector was on the scene.

It was clear that the thieves had broken the lock on the granary and shovelled the corn into sacks they brought with them. Then they carried them, three at a time, through the yard and into a corner of the meadow where a deep ditch bordered by a hedge had to be negotiated. It must have needed a lot of effort to get the sacks clear of these obstructions, but they made it, and went back for three more. They continued on with these three, clear across a ploughed field, heading for a cart they had waiting near a stile. But this was where they were challenged by the home-going policeman who had heard their noise in the darkness.

115

They dropped the sacks and turned on him. The sacks were knocked over in a frightful struggle and a lot of grain spilled out. The local paper described what happened: 'The murdered officer must have been felled to the ground on the outside edge of this greensward by the terrible blows he received on his head, and a scene of the most horrible butchery was then enacted, two large pools of blood, which on examination were found to contain hair, marking the spot where his throat was so savagely cut.'

It appeared in the light of day that the corpse must then have been carried to the ditch and dropped down into the water. Thrown in with the body were three sticks. One was Sergeant Eves's own stick, unscarred, showing he had been unable to use it in defence. The other two belonged to the robbers. One was a veritable bludgeon, cut out of the hedge, with a knob on it as big as a tennis ball. The other was splintered, showing the violence with which it had been smashed on the policeman's skull.

The robbers, no more than ignorant, illiterate labourers, then realised just what they had done. They panicked, went back down the field, picked up the sacks they had dropped and dumped them in a nearby pond, hoping to hide this evidence, but they forgot the sacks they had left poised above the ditch near the place where the dead policeman lay. It was shown later that they had then made their way to the Davis's house where they cleaned themselves up and tried to burn some of their clothing. By early Monday morning a trail of clues led to the arrest of four men — brothers John and 'Brickie' Davis, John Bateman and Charles Sales, the Davis's brother-in-law. They were about to set out for work at six in the morning when Inspector Pryke apprehended them. Some of the clothes they were wearing at that time were stained with blood, and it could be seen that efforts had been made to clean it off coats and boots. It was not until 11 am that John Bateman was arrested. All of them lived locally and each had rather feeble and rambling explanations to account for the bloodstains.

From this time the wheels of justice turned relentlessly and inevitably. The inquest was held on Tuesday and continued the following Monday. It concluded that Sergeant Eves was the subject of foul murder by persons at present unknown. From the intensive coverage of the murder by the local press we can sift the story of the dead policeman's character and career. A native of Hutton, he had joined the Essex Constabulary on 1st March 1877 when he was 20, after working as a wheelwright at Great Warley. He married the following year and the couple were moved about the county nine times from places as far apart as Southend and Harwich. In April 1891 they had come to Purleigh. Over the years he had earned several commendations in making difficult arrests and only the previous February had been promoted to the rank of Acting Sergeant.

A development in the case came when Thomas Choat walked into Maldon police station and incriminated James Ramsey, the driver of the threshing machine at Hazeleigh Farm granary and his son James, who also worked there as a chaff boy. The police took them into custody at once but the news spread so fast that before they had got these men back to Maldon police station a large crowd had gathered outside it. They fought for places in the tiny courtroom to hear that Ramsey senior had been heard using threatening language against Sergeant Eves at some time previous to the murder and his son, 15 years old, was said to have the type of knife which was said to have been used to cut the poor man's throat. He was not a very bright lad, he only increased suspicion of his guilt as he tried to cope with close questioning. Now there were six men languishing in prison awaiting further enquiry by the police.

The funeral and burial of Sergeant Eves was the next chapter in the story. Hundreds of people passed through his house to pay their last respects as he lay in state. His terrible wounds were hidden as far as possible. There were many emotional scenes. At the burial there were 'sobs and tears on all sides'. The police had already started a fund to pay for the erection of a suitably inscribed headstone. No less than 163 policemen were spared from duty to pay their last respects to their murdered colleague, whose coffin was borne by six sergeants with another six alongside carrying some of the many wreaths. The next day, Sunday, showed another side of public behaviour at such tragedy. The Queen's Head, Purleigh was besieged by hundreds of people for refreshments after travelling here in all kinds of conveyance. They flocked to the scene of the murder, to gape at the ditch and to pick up what 'souvenirs' they could, including grains of wheat and bits broken from the hedge.

The prisoners were lodged in adjacent single cells in Chelmsford prison and taken to the Maldon courthouse to be remanded several times while further evidence was searched for.

On 19th May the trial started with something of a sensation. The prosecuting counsel declared that he did not have sufficient evidence to put Bateman on trial and asked that he be discharged at once. He was then put in the witness box to tell on oath what Sales had told him during the long period on remand. Sales had confided to him, 'It's not much use me having a lawyer for I'm a guilty man.... What's the use of John and Richard (Davis) having a lawyer, for they're as guilty as I am.'

At this stage young James Ramsey was also eliminated from suspicion and was freed immediately. So the trial continued and on Friday 28th July the four men, John and Richard Davis, Charles Sales and James Ramsey went into the dock for the last time. For one of them it was a day of great rejoicing. As soon as Mr Justice Mathew was seated the prosecutor rose and said, 'My Lord, I have considered the matter in regard to the prisoner Sales, and I do not propose to press the charge against him.' So the jury there and then acquitted him. Sales was totally overcome with this unexpected turn of events and could only sob his thanks. When he left the dock his chair was removed and the three men left moved closer together.

Mr Scott, the Maldon surgeon, gave evidence on the wounds on the victim's body and how they might have been

Under the suspicion of the murder of Sergeant Eves were:
(top) James Ramsey Snr, James Ramsey Jnr, John Bateman
(bottom) John Davis, Richard Davis and Charles Sales.

inflicted. A spade owned by Richard Davis was put forward as an exhibit. He was convinced that at least two men were involved in the actual murder because Sergeant Eves, when on the alert, would have been more than a match for any one man. Various witnesses gave evidence as to the movements of the suspects over that weekend. Mr Crump the prosecuting counsel summed up his case, showing that no witnesses had been called for the defence; not one member of the family had come forward to confirm the movements of these men. The burning of their clothing had been confirmed by the finding of half-consumed trouser buttons. He sketched out the characters of the three men and suggested that what had started simply as a robbery ended horrendously in murder to prevent identification of the robbers.

The defence did their best, particularly concerning James Ramsey. The judge took one hour on his summing-up, and the jury took just about the same time to come to their verdict. They found John and Richard Davis guilty and James Ramsey not guilty. Ramsey simply walked out and down the street with his son, followed by a large crowd. Then the judge put on the black cap to sentence the brothers Davis to death by hanging.

The last words in this story were written by the *Essex Chronicle* in March 1989:

'Murdered bobby's memory honoured

Thirty years after the gravestone of murdered Purleigh police-man Adam John Eves was laid flat, it has been renovated and put back in place.

Purleigh's . . . village bobby PC Graham Ferris discovered the state the stone was in when the parish council surveyed all the graves in the churchyard. He thought more respect was due to someone who was killed in the line of duty and set about restoring the headstone to its former glory. Twelve months later the original piece of Portland stone has been cleaned and re-carved by a firm of Witham masons and replaced at a cost of £440, paid for by the Police Benevolent Fund.'

Index